THE PATHWAY OF ROSES

AUTHOR OF

The Ideal Made Real
On the Heights
The Hidden Secret
The Great Within
Mastery of Fate
How to Stay Young
Perfect Health
Poise and Power
Your Forces and How to Use Them
etc., etc., etc.

The Pathway of Roses

Christian D. Larson

DeVorss Publications
Camarillo, California

The Pathway of Roses
Copyright © 1911 by Christian D. Larson
Foreword/Introduction © 2005 by DeVorss & Company

All rights reserved. No part of this book may be reproduced, stored, or transmitted in any form without permission in writing from the publisher, except by a reviewer who may quote brief passages for review purposes.

ISBN 0875168140
Library of Congress Control Number: 2004116138
First Edition, 2005

DeVorss & Company, Publisher
P.O. Box 1389
Camarillo CA 93011-1389
www.devorss.com

Printed in the United States of America

Contents

Foreword

The Pathway of Roses and
Christian D. Larson's Journey in New Thought

by Jessica Hatchigan

Christian D. Larson, a former editor of *Science of Mind* magazine, and author of the 1912 bestseller, *Pathway of Roses*, was one of the most active proponents of New Thought in the first three decades of the 20th century, and was a strong influence on Ernest Holmes and on other influential leaders in religion and metaphysics.

Holmes struck up a friendship with Larson after he attended one of the lectures Larson gave each Thursday at the Wilshire Ebell Theatre in Los Angeles at the height of his career. Holmes visited Larson at his Beverly Hills home and even took a correspondence course with him.

Holmes was so impressed with Larson, he tried to convince him to start his own church. But Larson believed he was meant to express his message as a speaker and practitioner, and especially as an author.

Jessica Hatchigan (www.hatchigan.com) is an Ann Arbor-based freelance journalist and author. This article is reprinted from *Science of Mind* magazine, April 2005.

While he had no trouble speaking to large audiences, Larson was, in private life, generally deep in thought, and very much preoccupied with his writing, says his son, Christian Larson, Jr., a portrait photographer and photojournalist whose work has appeared in newspapers across the world. Larson, Jr. remembers his father as a man of profound faith, a gentle soul who liked routine. "He began every day by sweeping the driveway clean each morning, then went into his office and wrote.

"He was not an aggressive father, or the kind of dad who roughhoused or played ball with you," Larson, Jr., recalls. "He lived in a spiritual world, and he was very reserved. But in his quiet way, he was always there and always very, very responsive."

As a practitioner, Larson helped many who came to him. He must have been effective as Larson, Jr., remembers playing with his friends in front of the Larson home in 1934. The 10-year-olds watched as a limousine pulled up and Mae West—one of the best-known Hollywood stars of her day—stepped out, bedecked in satin and jewels for a consultation with his father. She opened her parasol and sauntered to the Larson home. "Mother shooed us away," Larson, Jr. recalls. But he and his friends enjoyed another memorable moment when, returning to her limo some time later, the star drawled, "See ya, boys."

Hollywood moments aside, Larson, Jr. recalls a very spiritually-centered home. "When issues arose," Larson, Jr. says, his father would quietly say, "We'll take care of that." Or, "We'll handle that." Or, most often, "We will demonstrate on that."

When the Larson family dog developed rabies, for example, "Father—showing no fear whatsoever—went to the dog and stroked it. Within 24 hours, the dog was cured." Another time, when warts appeared all over one of his son's hands, Larson, said, "We will demonstrate on that." Within a week the warts had all disappeared.

Larson, Jr. also recalls that when he was called into service during World War II, his parents prayed for him daily. Their prayers, he says, may have helped account for the fact that he was the only man in his unit—the 450th Bombardier Group— who came out of service unscathed.

Pioneer Roots

Larson's beginnings gave no hint that he would be a man Hollywood stars would one day call on. The third of seven children of newly-arrived Norwegian immigrants, he was born in 1874 in a pioneer dwelling, a log cabin built into the side of a hill on the family's Iowa farmland. The Larsons instilled their values— self-reliance and hard work—into their children. The family's fortunes steadily rose. Larson's older brother, Lawrence, would one day become head of the American Historical Society, and another brother, Edward, would become an inventor for Ford Motor Company.

The Larson children were raised as Lutherans and encouraged to think about the ministry as a profession. In 1894, Larson, urged by his parents, entered a Lutheran seminary. But on a train trip to the seminary in Minneapolis, a small but life-changing event occurred. A newsboy left a book by a Unitarian minister on the seat next to Larson. He bought the book, read it several times, and it became the catalyst for his break with orthodox theology. He completed his first year at the Lutheran seminary, but knew he would enroll in a liberal theological school the following year.

When he announced his decision to his parents, they refused to provide further financial assistance. But a wealthy banker in the community, learning of Larson's plans, applauded them and provided the money necessary.

By the time Holmes and Larson met in California, Larson had already established himself as a leading spokesman for New Thought. In 1901, at the age of 27, he'd launched *Eternal Progress*, which became a leading New Thought periodical of its day. The magazine was his vehicle to express his thoughts and ideas. In his unfinished autobiography, Larson describes how he saw himself—as one of the line of spokesmen for an ongoing evolution in American philosophical and metaphysical thought, an evolution that spanned back to the transcendental movement of the 1830's.

When a fire destroyed the Chicago building where *Eternal Progress* was published, rather than rebuild, Larson decided to "go west," and traveled to California, where Holmes first encountered him.

A prolific author, Larson wrote more than 40 books on New Thought themes. In his books, he offers thoughts and insights on the spiritual choices we make that determine the quality of our journeys through life. His emphasis was on the practical benefits right living could help manifest.

One of his best-selling books, *The Pathway of Roses*, from which many of the Larson quotations that follow are drawn, distills the essence of his teachings.

To Dream and to Do

In *Pathway*, Larson talks about three types of people.

The first type, he says, ignore spiritual realities and end up "merely existing."

The second "go to the other extreme," depending almost entirely upon power of spirit to provide supply. They "drift into adversity and want." These people are dreamers, Larson says, and generally don't achieve what they set out to do.

The third type, he says, have "unbounded faith" and are "disciples of work ... that adds to the welfare of the world." These are the dreamers who make their dreams come true.

And it all begins with spirit, Larson says. Each of us is made up of body, mind and soul. But it is "the life we live [in the soul that] we invariably bring forth into the mind and body."

The soul has this power to determine our external reality because it is that part of us that can tap into the divine. "The ills of personal life are not produced by divine will," Larson writes. "They are produced by man's inability to properly use that part of divine will that is being expressed in his mind." This inability stems from our being ignorant of, or deaf to, the spiritual part of ourselves that can help us to determine God's will for us.

But a willingness to do God's will doesn't mean we can have no goals of our own. Far from it. To get in harmony with divine will, Larson says, we need to "passionately desire to attain a worthy, lofty and specific goal." Relinquishment is a part of this, the willingness to say, "Thy will be done." But this doesn't equate to abdicating your own will, rather to "placing your own will and the whole of your life in oneness with God and in harmony with the divine order." This choice, Larson says, makes your own will right and infinitely stronger.

In Pathway, Larson equates living in God's will to "living on the heights" and living in ignorance of God's will to "living in the valley." When we live on the heights—when our spiritual self is correctly aligned to divine will—then our whole person—including the mental and physical aspects of us—will thrive. "When we do all things in the realization that we are spiritual beings filled with supreme power from on high, there is no limit to what we can do."

Mentor of Mentors

Many of Larson's teachings in *The Pathway of Roses* and his other books are familiar to us, because they have become truisms in self-help books.

Larson was one of the first, for example, to teach the principle of focusing your attention on what you hope to achieve, not on what you fear to lose. Always think that all is well, he advises. "Thus, that which is well, will manifest in every part of life, while that which does not seem to be well will pass away."

The mind, he urges, is to be absolutely focused on the good things we aim to build, establish and achieve. This mindset drives out fears and worries. Likewise, we are to pay as little attention as possible to negative thoughts and conditions and people. Deprived of our attention, these lose their strength and fade away.

Larson was one of the first to teach the power of affirmations, although he doesn't use that term. Instead he says, "Do not say that you will be in the future; say that you are now; and you are, because you are the exact image of the Supreme." Declaring a thing to be so, while aware of our connection to the divine, he tells us, helps manifest the things we desire.

And no matter how things appear, Larson advises, "say that life is beautiful." No matter how the body may feel, "say that you are strong and well." By speaking the truth you wish to create, you create it. "Say that you are well and you create health."

The same mindset of faith, he says, can overcome any failure.

The number of failures we experience are irrelevant, Larson says. We are never to label ourselves "weak," but to remember our true spiritual identity, the soul which is made in God's perfect image. "And the image of God is supreme strength." Even in the middle of sickness, failure, and poverty, we are to keep our focus on this absolute truth, and doing so will banish the negative conditions from our lives.

Giving in to discouragement and doubt alone can make failure final. Delays in achieving our goals require only steadfast recommitment to faith—even if the timetable for achievement is not what we hoped for. "Some of the greatest things in the world have been gained after many years of constant faith and prayer," Larson says. "What we ask for will come when our faith is right and our life prepared to properly use the great good desired."

Larson also taught the power of countering negativity with love and of refraining from anger and blame. When things are going wrong, he says, if we blame the world, we only feed negativity and empower it, "but when we love the entire world with the whole heart, the world will change toward us accordingly and be kind."

If we fail, if our businesses don't prosper, if there is no demand for our talents, Larson recommends two things: to continue our best efforts and to "love much." To get angry in the face of these kinds of disappointments is counter productive, he says. "When you do this you push the world further away from yourself."

As for those who mistreat us or speak wrongly against us, Larson warns that even the least bit of anger, indignation and negativity only attract, "disagreeable people and adverse conditions." The remedy? "Love those who have mistreated you; love them with the very deepest power of your soul and they will soon come to you to make everything right again . . . when you love everybody you attract only the best people and the best conditions." The love he speaks of, Larson emphasizes, is not the "weak, sentimental" kind, but "that strong soul-love that comes from the very heart of the Infinite."

While he warns against anger, Larson also warns against inaction. He was an advocate of action in going after what you want—action inspired by the confidence that God is with you. We are, he says, to ask God for the things we wish to achieve and have. "The best is intended for all of us," he writes, "God is ever ready to give everything . . . Whatever God may lead us to do He will always give us the power to do."

Larson adds that we can rely on God to lift us out of "poverty, trouble and pain," as these conditions are never God's will for us. And, he adds, "The Infinite can provide something better here and now, and it is His will and good pleasure to do so. . . . When days of darkness are at hand, cling to the great truth, spirit will provide."

One of Larson's most beautiful contributions to New Thought, is his emphasis on the simplicity with which each of us can connect with the divine, where all healings, inspirations, and blessings begin. "The key to the Scriptures is not some system of symbolical interpretation, nor some special method of metaphysical or spiritual analysis," he says. "The key is simply to enter the spirit when you begin to read. The spirit reveals everything that is sacred and true."

Christian Larson on Why We Are Here

Our purpose, Larson says, is to "live the purest, the largest, the fairest, the most useful, the most beautiful and the most spiritual life possible, just for today." We are to strive to be the best we can be today, at this moment. Our goal is not to compete against anyone else, but to be the shining soul we were created to be.

And we are to sew "good seeds" in the "garden of human life." It doesn't matter if we see them take root and grow. In fact, we may not actually see the fruits of our good works. But, knowing every well-intentioned action will have a good result, we can be happy in the knowledge that we have created happiness for others. "To feel that you have given happiness to someone else, is the greatest happiness of all; and to know that millions will be inspired by the sublimity of your life ages after you are gone— could anything give deeper joy to the soul?"

Certainly Larson's writings continue to inspire others, and the seeds he planted have created countless blooms on many a pathway of roses.

—JESSICA HATCHIGAN

Editor's Note

The Pathway of Roses, first published in 1912, endures as a beloved classic of New Thought literature. Its author, Christian D. Larson, was one of the most outstanding leaders of the early New Thought Movement, influencing such great teachers as Norman Vincent Peale and Religious Science founder Ernest Holmes. Since that time, this remarkable book has guided and uplifted countless readers throughout the years with its enlightened vision of spiritual Truth.

Larson had the dual gifts of clearly recognizing the transcendent power latent within all people and being able beautifully to express this elevating vision in words. *The Pathway of Roses* masterfully combines both of Larson's special gifts. Now in a long-awaited new edition, it is sure to continue to offer readers a rich treasure of spiritual understanding.

—KATHY JULINE, EDITOR

THE PATHWAY OF ROSES

To live always in the Secret Places of the Most High,
To think only those thoughts that are inspired
    from above,
To do all things in the conviction that God is with us,
To give the best to all the world with no thought
    of reward,
To leave all recompense to Him who doeth all
    things well,
To love everybody as God loves us, and be Kind as
    He is Kind,
To ask God for everything and in faith expect
    everything,
To live in perpetual gratitude to Him who
    gives everything,
To love God so much that we can inwardly feel that
    My Father and I are one,
This is the prayer without ceasing, the true worship
    of the soul.

CHAPTER I

Paths to the Life Beautiful

The thinking world of today is being filled with a phase of thought that has exceptional value. True, some of it is in a somewhat chaotic condition, but most of it is rich, containing within itself the very life of that truth that is making the world free. But in the finding of this truth, and in the application of its principles, where are we to begin? What are we to do first? And after we have begun, and find ourselves in the midst of a life so large, so immense and so marvelous that it will require eternity to live it all, what are the great essentials that we should ever remember and apply? What are the great centers of life about which we may build a greater and a greater life? These are questions that thousands are asking today, and the answer is simple.

First, recognize the great truth that every individual can live his own life exactly as he may desire to live. Man, himself, is the real master of his own existence, and he, himself, may determine how perfect and how beautiful that existence is to be.

Your life is in your own hands. You may live as you wish. You may secure from life whatever you desire, because there is no limit to life, and no limit to your capacity to live. The elements of life can be modified, changed, developed and perfected to comply with your own supreme demand; the increase of life can be realized in the exact measure of your largest need; you are in living touch with Infinite life, and there is neither limit nor end to the source of your supply.

To live in the constant recognition of this great truth, is to rise continually into higher and higher degrees of that mastery of life that gives man the power to live his life according to his most perfect ideals. To reach the goal that every ascending mind has in view, this truth, therefore, must ever be recognized and applied. It is one of those principles that we shall always require, no matter how high we may rise in the scale of divine being.

Second, desire that which you desire, and desire with all the power of mind and soul. We invariably receive what we desire, no more, no less. We get what we wish for if the power within that wish is as strong as we can make it.

The fact that we can have an ideal, proves that we have the power to secure it. The fact that we can formulate and appreciate a desire for something larger and better, proves that we can fulfill that desire. The great essential is to desire with the whole heart; that is, to give our desires all the life and power that we can possibly arouse from the depths of invincible being.

The true desire and the true prayer are synonymous. The true prayer is invariably some immensely strong desire expressed when the human mind feels the sublime touch of the Infinite mind; and the true desire must be in perfect touch with Infinite life in order to be filled with the invincible power of that life.

To cause every wish to come true, we must express all the power of mind and soul through every wish; but we cannot give expression to all the power within us until we awaken our spiritual natures, and we cannot awaken our spiritual natures until we begin to live with the Infinite. The largeness and immensity of the supreme spiritual life within us comes forth only as consciousness is spiritualized, and we gain spiritual consciousness by living and thinking constantly in the lofty state where we actually feel that God is closer than breathing, nearer than hands and feet.

We cannot desire too much, and when we desire with all the life and power that is within us, our desires shall positively be fulfilled. The wish must be whole-hearted, not half-hearted; it must contain all the power we have, not simply the limited actions of shallow thinking; and it must contain soul, not simply emotion, but that deep, spiritual feeling that touches the very spirit of limitless life and power.

Third, have faith in God, have faith in man, have faith in yourself, have faith in everything; and have faith in faith. When you have confidence in yourself you arouse everything that is stronger, greater and superior in yourself. In consequence, the more confidence you have in yourself, the more you will attain and accomplish. But the power of self-confidence is but an atom in comparison with the marvelous power of faith.

Faith takes mind and soul into the greater realms of life. It goes out upon the boundless, and awakens those interior spiritual forces that have the power to do anything. This is why all things become possible when we have faith.

It is the nature of faith to break bounds; to transcend limitations, and take life, thought and action into the universal. It is the nature of faith to unite the lesser with the greater, to unite the mind of man with the mind of God. Therefore, we shall always require faith; however far we may go into the greater, the superior and the boundless today, faith will take us farther still tomorrow. And that is our purpose; to realize our largest and dearest desires in the present, and then press on to the realization of other and far greater desires in the future.

Fourth, depend upon the superior man within for results, and give this greater man the credit for everything you accomplish. When you depend upon the personal self, you place yourself in touch only with the lesser forces on the surface; you therefore will accomplish but little; but when you depend upon the supreme spiritual self, you place yourself in touch with the greater powers within, and results will be greater in proportion.

When you give credit to the personal self, you ignore the interior spiritual man; you thereby fail to secure that greater wisdom and power that the spiritual man alone can supply. Instead of being led by that inner light that knows, you are led by the confusion of outer thought; you are turned away from the path that leads to truth, freedom and the perfect life, and your mistakes are many. Instead of being taken into the current of that invincible life that can carry you through to your very highest goal, you remain in the hands of mere physical energy, that energy that can do nothing more than simply keep your body alive.

Whenever you accomplish something worthwhile, and give the praise to your own outer personal self, you immediately lose your hold on those powers through which those results were gained; in consequence, failure will begin, and you will have to retrace all your former steps to again gain possession of that power that can do whatever you may wish to have done.

To constantly depend upon the greater self, to constantly expect the desired results from the greater self, and to always give credit to the greater self, is to constantly draw upon the limitless wisdom and power of the greater self, the supreme spiritual man within you. You thereby become larger and stronger in all the elements of your being, rising ever in the scale, gaining ground perpetually, and passing from victory to victory. What you desire you will receive because higher power is working through you, and as you ascend in the scale, there is nothing that you will not attain and accomplish.

The principal cause of failure among those who are trying to live in harmony with real truth, may be found in the general tendency to think of the outer person as the power that does things on the visible plane. But it is the interior man that gives the power, though the outer person is required to apply it. And the more thought we give to the interior man, the more life and power we bring forth from within.

The interior man is the man created in the image and likeness of God; it is therefore evident that when you begin to live with the life and the power of the interior man, the expression of real greatness and real spirituality will begin. And from that moment you will not be limited to the power of the personal self; instead you will fill the personal self with that divine power from on high that is limitless, inexhaustible and invincible.

Fifth, live for a great purpose, and hold the central idea of that purpose constantly before mind. Do not live for the mere sake of prolonging existence; live for something that magnifies, on the largest possible scale, all the elements of existence. To live for a great purpose is to live a great life, and the greater your life, the greater the good that you will receive from life. The ruling desire of every living soul is to have life, and have it more abundantly; therefore, to fulfill that desire we must continue perpetually to live for that which produces more life. No matter how rich we may become in the real, spiritual life, here is a principle that we must ever remember and apply.

Do not work for yourself; work for the great idea that stands at the apex of your greatest purpose. The greater the idea for which you work, the greater will be your work; and it is he who does the greatest work that does the most for everybody, himself included. When your work is great you become a great power for good among thousands, and at the same time you do more for yourself than you could possibly do in any other manner.

When you begin to live and work for a great purpose, you get into the current of great forces, great minds and great souls. You gain from every source; all the powerful lives in the world will work with you; you become a living part of that movement in the world that determines the greater destiny of man; you become one of the chief elements upon which will depend the future of countless generations yet to be; you become one of the chosen of the Most High.

To live for a great purpose is to live in the world of great ideas, and great ideas awaken great thoughts. Man is as he thinks. Great thoughts produce great minds; from great minds proceed great works, and great works constitute the building material with which the kingdom upon earth is to be constructed.

When we begin to live for a great and good purpose, we place in action that law that causes all things to work together for good. Henceforth, nothing is in vain; every person, thing or event that comes into our world will add to the welfare, the richness and the beauty of that world. All things become ministers of the life that is real life, we have been giving our best everywhere, and we are receiving the best from every source in return.

To live for that which is high, lofty and sublime, is to walk with God; the love, the life, the power and the wisdom of the Infinite will ever be with us, and to have such companions is to be blessed indeed. Every moment will give us the peace that passeth understanding, every hour will be filled with the joy everlasting, and every day will be as a thousand years in celestial kingdoms on high.

To give the world emancipation is the ruling desire of all minds that are spiritually awakened; and these should remember that to overcome evil with good is the only way. Forget the wrong that may appear in the outer world of things, and give all your thought to the great good that is inherent in all things. You thereby place in action the greatest emancipating power that the human race will ever know.

We are in bondage because we have lived to please the person. Follow the soul and freedom shall come quickly. Then we shall please the person better than ever before. To follow the soul is to enter the greater domains of life, those domains from which we may secure everything that is rich and beautiful and superior in human existence. The soul leads, not only into the life more abundant, but also into the actual possession of all the spiritual riches that the greater life may contain. And when we find the kingdom that is within, all that we may desire in the without shall be added.

The soul that lives most perfectly in the present, creates most nobly for the future. Be yourself today, regardless of what happened yesterday. Be all that you are or can be today, and you will live in a fairer world tomorrow.

CHAPTER II

The Way to Freedom

There is only one will in the universe just as there is only one mind. The one mind is the mind of God; the one will is the will of God. The mind of individual man is an individual or differentiated expression of the Infinite mind, and the largeness of this human mind depends upon how much of the one mind man may decide to appropriate. Man has the freedom to incorporate in his own individual consciousness as much of the Infinite mind as he may desire; and as the mind of the Infinite is limitless, the mind of man may continue to become larger and larger without any end.

The will of the individual mind is a partial expression of the will of God, just as the force of growth that is in each branch is a part of the same force that is in the vine, and the power of the individual will depends upon how perfectly the individual mind works in harmony with the Infinite mind.

There is no limit to the power of the will of God, the divine will; therefore, when the human will is as large a part of the divine will as the individual mind can appropriate and apply, the human will necessarily becomes immensely strong; and since the individual mind can appropriate a larger and a larger measure of the divine will, there is no limit to the power of will that can be developed in the mind of man.

To develop the true will, the first essential is to realize that there is but one will, and that we will with the one will just as we live the one life and think with the one mind, though in our thinking, living and willing, we do not, as a rule, do justice to that part of the whole which it is our privilege to use. We think, live and will too much as isolated entities instead of as divine beings eternally united with the Supreme.

The second essential is to realize that the divine will works only for better things and greater things. The path of the divine will is upward and onward forever, and its power is employed exclusively in building more lofty mansions for the soul. Therefore the will of God does not produce sickness, adversity or death; on the contrary, the will of God eternally wills to produce wholeness, harmony and life.

The ills of personal life are not produced by divine will; they are produced by man's inability to properly use that part of divine will that is being expressed in his mind, and his inability comes because man does not always apply his will in harmony with divine will.

When man uses his will as his own isolated power, he separates his mind more and more from the source of his power; in consequence, the power of his will becomes weaker, and he necessarily fails to accomplish what he has in view. He also falls apart from the one ascending current of life; he gets out of harmony with the true order of things, and sickness, trouble, adversity and want invariably follow.

The true use of the will is to apply the will in the full recognition of the oneness of the human will with the divine will. My will is as much of the divine will as I am using now, and it is my privilege to use as much of the divine will as I may desire. To constantly think of my will and the divine will as the same will, is to place my mind in such perfect harmony with limitless power of divine will that I can appropriate this power in larger and larger measure, and the more I appropriate, the stronger becomes the power of will in me.

When the individual mind is in such perfect harmony with the Supreme mind that the divine will can be given free and full expression, the will of the individual mind becomes invincible; the secret therefore of developing a powerful will is found here, and here alone.

The true will is never domineering nor antagonistic; neither does it ever apply the force of resistance. If you are antagonistic or have a tendency to resist everything that is not to your liking, it is proof conclusive that you are not in harmony with divine will. You are misdirecting your power, and are forming obstacles and pitfalls for yourself.

The divine will does not attempt to overcome evils and obstacles with antagonistic or domineering forces; the divine will does not fight wrong, it transforms wrong. It works in silence and serenity, but goes so deeply into the elements of things that it undermines the very first causes of all adverse or detrimental conditions. It does not resist the surface, but goes calmly beneath the surface and transforms those undercurrents from which surface conditions proceed.

The divine will, by going into the deeper life of all things, transforms all things into harmony with itself; and can transform all things because its power is supreme. Therefore when we are in the midst of adversity, we should not rail against fate nor antagonize those conditions that seem to work against us.

We have within us the power of divine will, and this will can change everything for good.

But it not only can, it will. It is not the will of God to keep any person in adversity. It is the will of God to set every person free, and every person will be set free when he places his life completely in the hands of divine will.

When the individual mind can say, from the heart, Thy will be done, the individual life has been placed in the power of divine will and that life will at once begin to pass out of adversity, sickness, trouble and want, into the world of freedom.

However, we do not give up our individuality when we give our mind over to divine will; we do not become automatons in the hands of some superior power; on the contrary, we open our minds to that power that alone can produce individuality. The individuality we now possess has been formed by whatever measure of divine will that we have incorporated in our own conscious existence, and by opening our minds completely to divine will, we shall gain sufficient power to make our individuality infinitely stronger and superior to what it now is. Our purpose is not to be used by the Supreme, but to use the power of the Supreme.

To live the life of God, think the thought of God, and will with the will of God—that is the secret path to the highly developed individuality; and it is such an individuality that becomes a master mind, a Son of the Most High.

When the individual mind declares, Thy will be done, consciousness must fully recognize the presence of Supreme power, and must realize, with depth of thought and feeling, that Supreme power invariably leads to higher ground, the world of freedom and superior existence.

When the mind gives up to divine will in an indifferent, submissive, self-surrendering attitude, it is not giving up to divine will; it is simply giving up to the surrounding forces of fate. Such a mind will permit the forces of adversity to have their way, thinking that it is the will of God that much suffering must still be endured, and will consequently drift with circumstances, accepting whatever comes as a necessary chastisement.

This method, however, weakens the mind, and places the individual more out of harmony with God than ever before. We always place ourselves out of harmony with God when we accept evil as coming from Him, and we weaken our own ability to use divine will when we permit adversity to exist thinking that it was sent from God.

To give the mind over to divine will is not to give up at all, in the ordinary sense of that term; we simply place ourselves in that position where we can use the power of the one true will instead of a mere imitation. We blend our own desires and aims with that power that we know can see us through, and we work in the realization that whatever is detrimental in our plans will be eliminated as we press on towards the great goal in view.

The mind that is aimless, waiting for the will of God to take him where he belongs, will drift with fate. He is not in the hands of divine will, he is in the hands of circumstances because he has not given divine will something to do. God does not tell us what to do; He has given us the wisdom to know our own desires and our own tendencies, and He has given us the power to fulfil those desires, but we must take individual action; this is why we have individuality and free individual choice.

However, when we do take individual action, God will work with us if we enter into harmony with Him, and when He is with us, failure is impossible.

To use divine will, we must first have a lofty purpose in view; we must have something high and something definite that we wish to attain; we must have something upon which to apply the limitless power of divine will, and we must desire to reach that goal with the very deepest and strongest desires of heart and soul.

Then we must will to press on, knowing that we are using divine will, the Supreme will of the Most High, because this is the only will in the universe. It is the will that eternally wills the higher, the greater and the better—the will that is invincible, and always does what it wills to do.

To the minds of the many the true meaning of the will of God has not been made perfectly clear; therefore the majority, even among those who have strong spiritual tendencies, hesitate to give up to the absolute direction of higher power. There is a slight dread in the mind of the average person whenever he thinks of entering the uncertainty and the mysteriousness of the seeming void, and as long as things are reasonably well he does not care to give up to some power he knows nothing of. And as a true understanding of higher power cannot be found among the many, there are, accordingly, but few who can actually declare, with the whole heart, "Thy will be done." We frequently pray for His will to guide us, nevertheless we inwardly expect to use our own wills in mostly everything we do. But such prayers are not true to the spirit, and therefore they prevent the soul from actually discerning the real meaning of God's will; and also prevent the mind from becoming a perfect channel for the expression of His will.

The universe is orderly from center to circumference, and everything is established upon the firm foundation of eternal right and universal good. There is a power that lives and moves throughout this vast immensity, and all those things that have a permanent place in the cosmos, or that are instrumental in any way in promoting the purpose of life, have their source in this one power. All the laws and forces in existence spring originally from this power; it is therefore the center and source of all that lives and moves; and this power is the will of God. Accordingly, to do the will of the Father is to enter into harmony with the universal order and promote the great eternal plan.

The laws of life are all expressions of Supreme will. God wills eternally the right and the true, and the act of His willing originates and perpetuates the sublime plan of life that harmoniously thrills the entire cosmos during endless eternities. God's will is constant and changeless; therefore all the laws and principles in existence remain ever the same, as they are all the expression of the One Will. All that we see in the life of the universe is the eternal coming forth of Divine Will, and the perpetual returning to the One Source.

The true will in every soul is an individualization of Infinite Will, and the true use of the individual will means the doing of the will of God. The Infinite Will does not seek to control things, but seeks eternally to give itself to things. And here lies the secret in correctly using the human will, and in placing the human will in perfect harmony with God's will. When you can say with the whole heart, "Thy will be done," you are not giving up your own will, but you are placing your own will and the whole of your life in oneness with God and in harmony with the universal order. Therefore, when you do the will of God your own will becomes right, and becomes infinitely stronger than it ever was before.

When we act in perfect accord with the laws of life on all the planes of being, we are doing the will of God because what we call law in life is the will of God in expression in life. He who lives in perfect harmony with nature, who fully appreciates her grandeur and her beauty, and who daily seeks to be inspired by the loveliness of her presence is doing the will of God in the natural world. He who rightly employs all the elements of mind and body, and who furthers the purpose of his own being in constant growth and unfoldment is doing the will of God in the human world. He who searches the deep things of God and enters into that high state where God becomes "closer than breathing, nearer than hands and feet"; he who lives and moves and has his being in the infinite sea of divine light, and ever ascends higher and higher into the greater glories of God's kingdom, is doing the will of God in the spiritual world.

Whoever can say with his whole heart "Thy will be done," has placed the whole of his life in perfect accord with God; and henceforth he will seek to live in perfect harmony with all that is, because all is of God. To do the will of God is not only to place one's life in the hands of God, but to be at peace with all the world, and to give one's whole life to all the world. The will of God seeks eternally to give itself to things, all things; the will of man, to be in harmony with the will of God, must do the same.

However insignificant a law may seem to be, it is God working in that part of His universe; and as He is everywhere, manifesting His power everywhere, we must live and work with Him in all things, even the most trivial, if we would be in perfect accord with His life and always do His will. A law in life is a path to greater things; in truth, an open door through which we may pass more closely into His presence. We can meet God at every expression of life, and whenever we are in the highest state of harmony with our expression of life, we have met God in that place. And also, when we use that expression of life in entering into a larger measure of life, we do the will of God in that place. Therefore, whoever meets God everywhere, and does His will in every place, will realize the fullness of life at all times and under every circumstance. And to realize the fullness of life is to realize the allness of the good.

The incompleteness of human life, in general, is caused by our failure to enter into perfect accord with all the laws in our sphere of existence. We may be wholly right in some things while the very opposite in other things. We may be scrupulous in regard to the right use of some laws, and at the same time continually negligent in regard to others. There are many who take perfect care of their bodies, and comply most rigidly with all known physical laws, yet they violate the laws of mind nearly every hour of their existence. Others are very careful so as to think only the truth, and do their best to remain continually in the most beautiful states of mind; but while aiming to live in mental ideals they are wholly indifferent to the welfare of the body. Not infrequently we find people who live in perfect accord with intellectual laws but violate daily the moral laws. Also, too many who are the reverse. In brief, the majority do the will of God in some realms while living entirely at variance with His laws in other realms. And here we find the simple answer to many perplexing questions.

When some misfortune comes to you that you do not think you deserve, do not think that God is unjust or that fate is unkind. You have simply failed to do His will in all things. Do not blame others, do not blame fate, do not even blame yourself; simply proceed to readjust your life so that you may become one with Him in all things. Then all ills shall disappear, and you shall not only regain what you have lost but you shall, in addition, receive much more. Live in accord with all the laws of life physically, mentally and spiritually; do all things in the consciousness of God; do all things to the glory of God, and follow the light of His spirit in every thought and deed; then you will always do the will of God.

Though you may dwell upon the mountain tops of the spirit, though you may glory in the splendors of the cosmic realm, though your mind may go out upon the vastness of the limitless and your soul ascend to empyrean heights, still, do not for a moment deprive the body of anything that is rich and beautiful in physical existence. The great goal is the spiritual life, and in the spiritual life all the joys of sense, all the joys of intellect and all the joys of the highest heavens are divinely blended into one. The physical life is sacred. The earth is the foot-stool of the Most High. God lives in His heaven, but every atom in the visible universe thrills with the glory of His radiant presence.

CHAPTER III

The Supreme Point of View

When we are upon the mountaintop of life and look upon things from this lofty point of view, we discover that all is well. Wherever we may turn our vision we find the same—all is well. We can see all things and yet all is well with all things; the good alone is in evidence; everything is in the likeness of God, and we conclude that everything actually is as it was originally created by God—very good.

But when we descend to the valley we find many things quite different, and the problem is whether the scene on the mountaintop was simply a beautiful vision, or the scene in the valley an unpleasant illusion.

To the mind in the valley the life of the valley alone seems real; to the mind on the heights the beauty and glory of sublime life alone seems real, while the regions below are but the undeveloped beginnings of some better day.

To decide which of these two minds is right is not necessary; we cannot know the truth by what seems to be true from a single point of view. It is results that demonstrate; therefore we must find what effect life in the valley has upon the whole of life, and what effect life on the heights has upon the whole of life.

To live in the valley alone, ignoring everything that may come from lofty realms, is to live in darkness, trouble and pain. This we know. To him who secludes himself in the lower regions of existence, nothing seems to be wholly well; there is usually something wrong or defective with everything with which he may come in contact, and life at best has but little to give.

How different, however, everything becomes when we begin to live on the heights. We not only find that all is well in these upper regions but all things become well in the lower realms the moment we begin to live in the upper. We must therefore conclude that all is well when we are well, but that we are not well unless we live on the heights.

We also conclude that the vision of the soul is true, that the ideal alone is real, and that man can see all things as they are only when entering sublime existence. And as all is well from the viewpoint of sublime existence, to think the truth man must always think that all is well.

To live in the lower realms is to live in pain; to live in the upper realms is to live in peace, freedom and joy. Then why should we continue to live in the lower, while wholly ignoring the upper? Why should we declare that the lower alone is real, and that the upper is but a pleasant dream? Is pain more real than joy? Is bondage more real than freedom, death more real than life?

True, daily experience sometimes seems to contradict the vision of the soul, but if darkness be present now, does that prove that light is always a mere dream? When we are wholly out of harmony we cannot understand, for the time being, how there can be any harmony; all seems to be discord; but the moment we fully recognize the absoluteness of universal harmony, discord is no more.

When all does not seem to be well in daily life, we may not feel that we can truthfully say that all is well, but there is a marked distinction between the outer appearance of discord and the inner reality of harmony; and it is the inner reality that we should live.

When discord appears on the surface, the cause may be found in the fact that we have descended from our true place; we have tried to go away from harmony and have thus produced discord. But the moment we return to harmony, the discord disappears, and all is well.

We must conclude, therefore, that so long as we remain in the reality of harmony, all will be well, because all is always well in the world of harmony, and the world of harmony is the true world, the only true world—the world in which man was created to always live.

And we must remember the great truth that so long as man lives in the world of harmony there can be no discord anywhere; so long as he lives in the upper regions nothing can go wrong in the lower regions. The lower states of life are but effects of what man does, and when man is on the heights he will do only that which is well because all is always well on the heights; therefore, since like causes produce like effects, all will be well in the valley so long as man lives on the mountaintop.

This being true, every person should always think that all is well, and should always live in that sublime life where all is absolutely well. Thus, that which is well, will manifest in every part of life, while that which did not seem to be well will pass away. Live in the true, and the whole of life becomes true.

Whoever discerns clearly the spiritual essence or divine substance which is the basis or soul of all reality, will manifest in the form, not only purity, but absolute immunity from all disease and from all adverse actions among physical elements and forces. His body will be spiritualized in proportion to this understanding, and will establish itself more and more firmly in that state of being where divine nature reigns supremely. To spiritualize the body is to give greater strength, more perfect health and more youthful vigor, as well as higher quality, to the body. To establish the body in the consciousness of the spirit is to give the body absolute protection from weakness or disease; in the spirit we find all the elements of perfect being for body, mind and soul, and we place the body in the spirit when we realize that every atom in the body is filled, through and through, with the real substance of spirit.

Make yourself a living example of the power of spirit. Do not permit a single weakness to continue for a moment. Do not say that you will be in the future; say that you are now; and you are, because you are the exact image of the Supreme.

CHAPTER IV

The True Order of Things

What the individual life is to be, as a whole, or in any of its parts, depends upon where the consciousness of being is established, and there are three distinct planes in which this consciousness may be established; viz., the physical, the psychical and the spiritual.

To establish life in the physical is to become a materialist; there will be no consciousness of the finer things of existence, and the understanding of things in general will be one-sided; in consequence, the mind cannot see anything as it really is, and will make mistakes at every turn.

The materialist lives for the body alone, and depends upon the physical senses exclusively, both for knowledge and enjoyment; but the physical senses are never wholly reliable unless when employed by mental faculties that are above the physical; therefore the knowledge of the materialist is composed principally of illusions and half-truths, and his enjoyment is but an inferior imitation of real happiness.

The life of the materialist is necessarily full of troubles and ills because he cannot be in harmony with the true principle of life so long as he is living on the surface of life instead of in real life itself. In brief, all the ills of life can be traced to materialism, in one or more of its various forms; therefore, the materialist is not simply one who denies the existence of the soul; the materialist is any one who lives in the body, who has established his life in physical existence, and who employs objective senses and faculties only, regardless of what he may believe about God, the soul or the future.

Though a person may be thoroughly religious, as far as he knows, and may believe everything that sacred literature may say about things spiritual, if he cannot comprehend the spiritual except as it is expressed in physical acts, physical ideas, physical rites or physical symbols, he is still a materialist; he is living in the world of tangible things, and has no consciousness of that higher power that produces things.

To be spiritual he must discern the spirit that is within things, back of things, above things; while his senses admire the outer symbol, his spiritual discernment must understand the interior significance of that symbol, otherwise he has not found real religion or real spirituality.

The mind that has not entered into real spirituality is living in materiality, and to live in materiality is to be in bondage to the ills of this world; therefore true existence cannot be realized so long as life is established in the physical plane.

To establish life in the psychical plane is to be guided almost entirely by feeling and emotion; but no feeling is absolutely true unless it originates in the soul, and our feelings cannot originate in the soul unless we have established life in the spiritual plane. Therefore, the person who is living in the psychical plane is living in a world of feelings, emotions, desires and sensations that are more or less abnormal. His mental world is artificial, composed principally of imaginations that are patterned after things from without instead of the understanding of absolute truth from within.

The imagination is always influenced a great deal by the play of the emotions; and when the emotions are the results of external suggestions, as they always are unless when we live in the spirit, the imagination will likewise be under the control of things, good and otherwise. This means that our thinking will be worldly, materialistic and more or less disordered, because as we imagine, so we think.

Therefore, to live in the psychical world is to live in a world of abnormal feeling and misdirected imagination; but true being cannot find its foundation in such a world. True being can be established only in the consciousness of truth, and the consciousness of truth can be gained only in the spirit.

When life is established in the spiritual state, the physical ceases to be materialistic, and the psychical ceases to be a troubled sea of conflicting emotions. Instead, the physical becomes an orderly expression of the pure, wholesome life of the soul, and the psychical becomes a world of the richest thought, the most sublime feeling and the highest mental enjoyment.

The spiritual state of being is the true foundation of being, because the spiritual alone has the necessary qualities. To establish life in any other state or upon any other plane is to act contrary to the true order of things, and trouble must necessarily follow. There is only one place for man to live, and that is in the soul. When he tries to live elsewhere, in mind or body, he separates himself from his great inheritance and does not receive what he has the right and the privilege to receive.

When there seems to be nothing in life, the fault lies with the man himself, not with the laws of his being. Instead of living in the spirit, where he could receive everything, he has gone to live in the emptiness of the material, where there is nothing to be had but the undesirable consequences of wrong-doing; and wrong-doing is the direct result of wrong-going, going away from the true state of being.

To live in the spiritual state is to give expression to everything that is in the spirit, because what we actually live we bring out into tangible existence; and the spirit contains everything that may be required to perfect the whole of existence—physical, mental and spiritual.

The belief that the spiritual life is apart from the mental and physical is not true; it is the spiritual alone that can make the physical and the mental complete; in brief, we do not begin to enjoy the body and the mind until we begin to live in the soul.

We cannot attain the most perfect physical health and the most perfect physical development until we can begin to draw upon the inexhaustible life of the spirit, nor can we attain the greatest intellectual power and the highest mental brilliancy until our minds are opened to real spiritual illumination.

To have health and wholeness of body, we must have an abundance of that life that is health and wholeness, and that life comes only from the soul. To gain that life we must live in the soul, and the life that we live we invariably bring forth into mind and body.

To perfect the beautiful in the physical form, we must, likewise, receive the necessary elements from the spiritual state. Beauty of form is produced by harmony in formation and soul in expression; but we can give forth neither harmony nor soul until we actually live in the soul.

The true development of mind, character and life, all depend upon our ever-increasing expression of the perfect qualities of the spiritual life; therefore the truest, the best and the greatest results from physical existence and mental existence can come only when we actually enter spiritual existence.

But to enter the spiritual is not simply to provide those essentials through which we may realize the ideal in the physical and the mental; to enter the spiritual is to enter another and a greater world—the transcendent kingdom of the soul—the sublime world of cosmic consciousness. It was into this world that Jesus entered when "his face did shine as the sun and his garment became white as the light." We can therefore imagine what is in store for those who open their eyes to its splendor and glory.

"Be not therefore anxious for the morrow. Sufficient unto the day is the evil thereof." The term "evil" signifies incompleteness, or that which needs perfecting, development and fulfillment now. The statement therefore means that we have sufficient to do to make the present moment full and complete, without giving any thought to what we are to be or do in the future. When the present moment is filled with the most perfect life that we can possibly realize, the seeming incompleteness of the present moment will simply become a perpetual growing process. Incompleteness will thus become a real step in growth; it will be like a growing bud, and will not be evil, only lesser good on the way to greater good. When the bud ceases to grow it decays, and becomes unwholesome, disagreeable. Likewise, when the buds in human life are checked in their growth they produce disagreeable conditions. And here is the cause of all the ills of the world. The remedy is to so live that all the power of life is centered upon the present moment. To give the whole of life to the present moment is to promote the growth of everything that exists in the life of the present moment. To live a full life now is to live more and more life now.

CHAPTER V

The Good That Is In You

The good that is inherent in everything is infinitely greater and more powerful than any imperfection or undeveloped condition that may exist in the outer world. And therefore when this good is recognized and brought out into real life, that which is not good must disappear. To apply this great truth to yourself, to others, to circumstances, is to place mind and soul in that attitude where conscious contact with the divine perfection in all things will be gained. In consequence, the good that is within will increase, while undesired conditions in the without will decrease. To recognize the greater good that is inherent in all things is to cause that good to become a greater and greater power in you, until it becomes just as strong in action as it previously was in realization.

Live in the conviction that "I am greater than all my ills or failures; that I am greater than the limitations of my circumstances, and greater than any condition that I can possibly meet." When you feel that you are greater than your ills, those ills cannot long remain, because what you inwardly feel, you realize, and what you realize, you bring forth into living expression. To open the

29

mind to the great thought that the health that is within you is greater than any disease than you can ever know, is to open your life to the power of that health; and when the greater power of the health that is within you comes forth into the life of every atom in your being, the lesser power of disease, weakness or adverseness must vanish completely. No disease can long remain in your system after you begin to live in the constant conviction that the absolute health that is within you is infinitely greater and more powerful than all the sickness in the world. Nor can failure continue after you begin to realize that you, in the reality of your whole being, have the power to turn the tide of any circumstance that may ever appear in your world. The good that is within you is larger and more powerful than all the troubles, misfortunes or disappointments in existence; and this good, when fully recognized by you, will begin to work for you. It will work for your good, and will turn to good account everything that can happen.

When you know that you are greater than any undeveloped condition that may exist in mind or body, you gain the power to transcend limitations. Your consciousness begins to break bounds, and you find yourself in that larger, richer mental world that you so long have desired to reach. You are placed in touch with the universal and begin to draw upon the limitless for wisdom and power and joy. You no longer feel cramped, but realize that you are absolutely free to live the largest, the best and the most beautiful life that you can possibly picture. The ideals that you discover during the highest flights of mind and soul are no longer considered impossibilities; you know that you can realize them all; to you there is no failure because the good that is within you is greater than all failure. You are above limitations; you are master of limitations and have the power to transform every undeveloped condition into the highest form of completeness and superior worth. The lesser is passing away, and the greater is being realized in an ever increasing measure.

The good that is inherent in others is infinitely greater than all their faults, short-comings or imperfections; therefore we can readily forgive them for all these. There is more in man than the undeveloped surface, and it is this more that we will recognize, love and admire. When anyone goes wrong we will not criticise or complain; we cannot criticise anyone without harming everybody concerned, ourselves included; nor can we think well of anyone without helping everybody concerned, ourselves included. And everybody wants the best to happen to everybody. To live in constant recognition of the weaker side of human nature is to open the mind to weakness, discord, failure and unhappiness. We steadily grow into the likeness of that which we think of the most. But to live in constant spiritual touch with the great good that exists in everybody is to open the mind to strength and happiness that cannot be measured. The most beautiful. moments in life are realized when we feel that we are one with God and one with that something in man that is created in the image of God. And these moments may become eternal.

Whatever we may meet in life we should always remember that the good within all things is far greater than anything that may appear on the surface; and that this greater good will finally rule the day. When this good is to reign supremely in our world will depend upon us and us alone. The superior within us is always ready and will come forth into tangible expression whenever we are ready to receive it. But we are not ready until we give the greater good in all things the first thought, no matter what the circumstances may be. Whatever may come, meet it all with the thought that the good within is greater still. The good that is inherent in all things is always greater and more powerful. The greatest things in the without are insignificant in comparison. Therefore, we can readily understand how easily the circumstances and conditions in the external world could be changed for the better, provided the all-powerful good within us was called forth into tangible action. And now we smooth the pathway of life when we realize that there is a greater good in everything we meet. How kindly we feel toward all persons and all events; nothing seems adverse any more and what we previously looked upon as obstacles are now stepping stones in attainment. By recognizing the greater good in all things, we open our minds to the wisdom and the power that is contained in this greater good; and, in consequence, we are inspired by every circumstance and enriched by every experience. We gain something from everything we pass through, and every event, however adverse, simply tends to arouse more and more of the real greatness within. Even evil, in all of its forms, becomes a lifting power in our world, because we are in constant touch with the great good that is back of and above all evil. We are not crushed by the ills and the wrongs that may exist about us, but instead we are inspired to greater thoughts, greater deeds and a greater life. All things serve us because we have found that greater good in all things that is ever waiting to serve. We have become friendly with the best that is in the world, and the best is becoming friendly with us in return.

The great and good are many, but he who loves with such a love that with his love some other soul has scaled the heights and there beheld what life eternal holds in store for man, has wrought the noblest of them all. Then give me such a love in boundless measure. Give me the love of some inspired soul whose living presence, fair and strong, can spur me on and on to greater heights than human life has ever reached before—some pure and tender heart who knows the sacred longings of that life supreme within that must ascend and evermore ascend—some fair illumined soul whose spirit dwells within the vision of transcendent realms on high and knows that I am made for such a place. Then life shall be a life indeed to me; my sacred longings all shall be fulfilled, and every good that I can wish for shall be mine, for all the joys of earth and all of heaven's ecstasies sublime abide for evermore in such a love.

CHAPTER VI

Give Your Best to the World

We have looked far and wide for remedies, but in our search we have overlooked one of the greatest of all; and that is love. Not the love of the person; not mere sentiment or emotion, but that strong, spiritual feeling that makes every atom in your being thrill with the purest sympathy and the highest kindness; and that makes you feel that every creature in existence deserves your most tender care and attention.

When everything goes wrong with us, we blame fate, environment or the world; we forget that the world does to us what we have done to the world. When we blame the world for everything, the world will so act that it will be to blame; but when we love the entire world with the whole heart, the world will change toward us accordingly and be kind.

When you do not succeed, when no one seems to care for your service, or for your talents, there are two things to do; do your best and love much. Do not condemn the race because it is slow to appreciate your worth; when you do this you push the world further away from yourself, and its appreciation will decrease instead of increase. Love the world, the whole world, and love with all the power of heart and soul; this will bring the world nearer to you; you will enter into friendly relationship with the world; the race will thereby discover what you have to give and will come at once to receive your talent.

True achievement in any sphere of action depends upon real ability, and a strong, deep, whole-souled love. Real ability can be cultivated, and we can all learn to love much; therefore the future of any person may become far greater and more beautiful then the present.

When others speak wrongly against you, do not permit the slightest trace of ill-feeling; anger and indignation not only weaken your own system, but also cause you to attract disagreeable people and adverse conditions. Love those who have mistreated you; love them with the very deepest power of your soul and they will soon come to you to make everything right again. Love can change the worst hatred into the deepest love; and what is more, when you love everybody you attract only the best people and the best conditions.

Love much, and lovely souls will daily come into your life; and those people who are not as lovely as they might be, will become better because they have met you and felt the divine fires aflame in your soul.

When people are going wrong, just love them; not with the person, nor in a weak, sentimental sense, but with that strong, soul-love that comes from the very heart of the Infinite. Such love will lift anybody; and whoever is lifted up into the better becomes better. When we ascend in the scale of life we enter the truer and the higher; we enter the right and thereby become true and right.

When you have reason to think that others are trying to take advantage of you, have no fear. Do not condemn; do not think of the wrong they are planning to do; take God with you and love them; love as you never loved before, and the wrong they are holding against you will change and become a great power for your good instead. Love can change any condition or circumstance and every change that comes through love is a change for the better.

Love brings us into right relations with all persons and all things; love removes inharmony, perverted feelings, obstacles, barriers and all kinds of unnatural conditions, and produces that perfect oneness through which the beautiful life can come forth. He who has placed himself in oneness with man can easily find his unity with God; but no one can find God who does not love man. When we love the whole race with the whole heart, then we shall enter the presence of Him who is love.

It is the truth that "He is nearest to God who is nearest to man"; and the nearer we are to God, the more life and power we receive from above; in consequence, the more we can accomplish in the world, and the better off will the world be because we came here to live for a while.

To be at peace with everything is one of the greatest secrets to greatness, usefulness and high spiritual attainment; and he alone can find the peace that passeth understanding who loves everybody and loves much. But true spiritual love does not love because it expects to gain thereby; when we love in the spirit of gain our love is only material emotion, and does not come from the spiritual depths of the soul.

Pure soul love loves because it is love, and must love. It loves because it is its very life to love, and could not cease loving without ceasing to be. And it cannot cease to be because the love that is love is eternal love. Therefore to awaken the love of the soul is to place in action one of the highest powers in the universe; a power that can do so much because it is so much.

To feel the interior presence of this love, with its high, strong, invincible power, perfectly blended with the sweetest tenderness, not only produces a joy that cannot be measured but also lifts you into a universe that is fairer by far than we ever imagined heaven to be. And truly it is heaven we enter when we love with such a love, when we love as God loves.

Pure love sees no evil, no sin, no wrong; it does not live in the world of illusion or darkness; it is a child of the light and radiates its spiritual glory wherever it may be. Where love is, there will the light be also; and neither darkness, sickness nor sin can exist in the light.

There is nothing that will not be blessed by the presence of love; and the soul that loves with the spirit, that loves much and loves always, will meet the good alone. He has given his best to the world, and the world will open its heart to him and be kind.

As the years pass by, the world will lavish upon him the richest treasures within its power to give, and nothing will be too good to place at his door. Blessings of all kinds from every direction will come in greater and greater abundance, and his life will be full with the best that God and man can give; because he has given his best to the world, and loved much.

The practical mind may think that this is only sentiment, and therefore has no value, neither for the physical life nor for the spiritual life. But too often the practical mind looks for his treasure in the realm of effect instead of in the realm of cause; in consequence, he finds but little of real value anywhere in life. The great things in life do not come through minds that dwell merely on the surface, that cannot rise above the world of tangible results. Everything that is beautiful and of real worth, whether it appeals to the eye, the ear, the intellect or the soul, has come through the mind that had visions, the mind that could soar to supreme heights, and behold the real splendor and glory of the world.

To be practical is well and necessary; but there is something else that comes first. This something else brings forth the substance, the material upon which practical efforts may be applied; therefore, the practical mind cannot act until the dreamer has had his vision.

The higher nature of man must act before the external mind can find anything of value to do; the soul must live and think before the person can attain and achieve, and the greater the love, the greater the life and the thought of the soul.

Whatever has added to the welfare of man in any age has been the product of the mind with the vision. All the good things of life have come from the world of visions and dreams. Someone entered the finer realms of life for a moment and brought back a treasure. The practical mind turned it to use, and the world was richer and better than it was before.

This being true, it is the very height of wisdom to train ourselves to enter consciously and frequently into those finer realms and thus bring forth more of its hidden treasures. It is the best we all seek, and since the best comes from the ideal world, the better we understand the ideal, the richer and greater life will become. To be practical in the largest sense of that term is to so live that we can touch the sublime on the one hand and turn every ideal into a living reality on the other.

The great mind is the dreamer, the prophet, the soul with visions; the mind that can soar to empyrean heights and reveal to the race some higher truth, some better way, and thereby elevate the whole of mankind. This is the mind that brings real values to the world, that makes life worthwhile; and one of his principal secrets is love.

When we love in this supreme, spiritual sense, we give a power to our practical efforts that we never gave before. We give life to our work; we do more and better work; results double and more; we do this through a power that many ignore as mere useless sentiment; and we thus demonstrate that love, the deep, strong, soul love, is as practical as any tangible force in the world.

There is nothing to lose but failure, and everything to gain, when we learn to love in this strong, high, universal sense. To begin, love as much as you can; be directly interested in the highest welfare of everybody; feel in the depths of the soul that we are all working together for the greatest good to all the race; and make this feeling so strong that it thrills every fibre in your being.

But do not love for effect; love because you feel love; and train yourself to feel love by loving with all the power of love, and in the highest, purest sense you know. He who tries to ascend will go up; he who tries to become strong will enter power; and he who tries to love everybody with the deepest, highest, strongest love of the soul will daily enter more and more deeply into the very spirit of that love that is love. And when you are awakened in the world of true spiritual love, real love takes possession of all your feelings and desires; and all your love will eternally love because it is love. From that moment you will constantly receive love from all the world and constantly give love to all the world. You will gain possession of one of the highest and one of the greatest powers in the universe, and the Infinite will always be with you. God is with every soul that loves much; because it is love, the deep, pure, spiritual love that gives man the power to know that My Father and I are One.

When there is anything you truly wish for, do not stand passively hoping that something may happen to make your wish come true; go out and make that wish come true; have the faith that you can; believe in the power that God has given you and God will give you more. Know that all the good in the universe lies in the path of him who has faith, and who will use the power of faith to make his own faith come true. He who only hopes will see visions of good things but will never reach them. But he who transforms his hope into faith and his faith into living works, will reach every lofty goal he has in view. To him nothing shall be impossible, for God is with him.

CHAPTER VII

Giving Much and Receiving Much

When you have attained or received something of exceptional worth, give God the glory. Do not praise yourself or give your own personality the credit. All power comes from above, and the more we appreciate the source of this power the more we shall receive. The path to perpetual increase is to give God the glory for everything that comes, and when we realize that everything comes from God, everything that comes to us will have exceptional worth. Every moment will be a demonstration of the power of truth, every experience will be an open door to a larger, more beautiful world, and every person, thing or event that we may meet, will add to our welfare and joy. With God all things are possible, and when we give Him the glory for everything we are with Him in everything.

To live the life of the great eternal now in the consciousness of those spiritual elements in which the real man lives and moves and has his being, is to enter the new heaven and the new earth. In the spirit all things are forever new, and the life of the spirit is perpetual ascension into the newer, the larger, the more beautiful, the more sublime. When life seems barren and useless, we are not in the spirit, but the moment we enter the spirit, a million universes are revealed to mind, and the joy of existence becomes supreme. We are not required to search the world of things for happiness, worth, entertainment or events of interest; one moment in the spirit is far more interesting than a whole life of physical existence, and one hour in the cosmic world is a thousand ages of unbounded bliss.

Depend upon the Infinite and His power will see you through. We learn that the Lord fought for Israel in ages gone by, and he will do the same now, for He changeth never. The term "Israel" means one chosen of God, and every person who chooses to go with God will be chosen of God. Go with God, live with God, walk with God, depend upon God in all things, and you will be chosen of God. When you choose God as your leader and your King, He will fight your battles; He will be with you always, and you will never see anything but victory. We fail only when we depend upon ourselves, ignoring the presence and the goodness of the Supreme. We go wrong only when we follow the light of our own darkness, forgetting that the guiding light of the Most High is at hand. This light knows what we ought to do, and when we follow this light we will always do that which is best.

The light of the spirit never leads into sickness, trouble or want. The light of the spirit invariably leads out of that which is evil and into that which is good. To go with God is to go into freedom, into happiness and into everything that can add to the richness and beauty of life. God is rich and can give us everything we may need without depriving anyone of anything; and when God leads us on to victory no one will lose because we have gained. The best will happen to everybody, and the greatest good will come to all. The gain of one is the gain of the many, providing that gain was secured through higher power; and when the one ascends in the scale, millions will discover the light they so long have desired to see.

This is our purpose: To live the purest, the largest, the fairest, the most useful, the most beautiful and the most spiritual life possible, just for today. To be our very best here and now, with no desire to outshine some other being, but simply to be all that we are in divine being now. To fill the present moment with all the spiritual sunshine that we can possibly radiate through the crystal walls of love, peace, faith and joy; and to live so near to the Supreme that we may touch the hem of His garment whenever we so desire. This is life, and he who lives with such a purpose forever in view shall never know an undesired moment.

To believe in the Christ is to enter into the Christ consciousness; not simply to believe something about what He was, but to realize what He is; to feel the sublime life that He felt and to know that touch of the spirit that He knew. We believe in the Christ only when we can mentally feel the power of His life in our own divine nature, and we believe in His name, the name that is above all names, when we can inwardly discern the full spiritual significance of that name. Belief in the Christ is not of the letter, but of the spirit; not to be definitely expressed in words, but to be inwardly felt in the soul. To ask in the name of the Christ is to enter into the spiritual understanding of that name, into the very soul of the power of that name, and in that sublime state offer our prayer. When we enter into that realization where we know what the name of Christ signifies in the spirit, we can ask in His name; and what we ask in His name we invariably receive.

When we enter into the spirit of the name of the Christ we are in the supreme power of the Christ; we inwardly know what the

Christ is and what He can do; and being in His power, we are in that power that can do and will do whatever we wish to have done. We fail to receive only when we are outside of that power that can give; but we invariably enter into the power of the Christ when we inwardly know the spiritual meaning of His name. To end a prayer by simply saying, "We ask it in Christ's name" is not sufficient; we ask in His name only when we can consciously feel that divinity that is defined by the name of the Christ. Words have no power unless they are spoken in the feeling of the spirit of that truth that the words are intended to convey. We speak to God only when we spiritually discern and inwardly feel what we say, and God answers only those prayers that are spoken to Him.

We should never try to eliminate evil. To resist evil, to give thought to evil, or to work against evil, is to give more life and power to the very thing you wish to remove. Overcome evil with good, but do not array the good against the evil, thinking that overcoming implies resistance or warfare. To overcome is to rise out of, forgetting the lesser by giving the whole of life to the greater. The purpose of life is to grow eternally into the greater good. Aim to fulfill this purpose and evil of every description will disappear. There is no wrong in the world that demands our attention. The good alone deserves our attention, and when the good receives all our attention, evil cannot exist any more. Build for the right; inspire every soul with an irresistible desire for the right, and everything you do will add to the power that makes for freedom. Think of the good, speak of the good, work for the good, live for the good, and the good only, and your life will be a light wherein darkness can never be.

The false prophet always predicts evil, trouble, misfortune and death. He can see only the weak side, the man made, the coming and going illusions. The true prophet can see that which lies behind the illusion, that which is possible, that which is in store, that which can be done and will be done. He keeps the eye single upon the high state, and thereby ascends into the reality of that vision which previously seemed but a dream. Every person who judges according to appearances is a false prophet; he forms conclusions that are not true to real life, and by following those conclusions causes that which is false and undesirable to come to pass. Every person who judges according to the divinity that is inherent in man is a true prophet; he brings truth into expression and thereby causes that which is true to prevail in tangible existence. The true prophet can see the greatness, the beauty and the perfection of the soul of man, and knowing that the soul is the master, predicts the coming of everything that is in the soul or that the soul has the power to do; and all such predictions will come true.

God is sufficient. When you are in sickness, trouble, sorrow or want depend upon the Supreme. You need nothing else. Infinite power is greater than all power, and if you have perfect faith, this power will surely set you free, no matter what the condition of bondage may be. The ills of the world continue principally because we think that something else besides the Infinite is required. But to depend upon other things besides the one is idol worship. The true worship of God, the highest worship of God, is to live so near to God that we can, at all times, feel that power that can do everything, will do everything, is doing everything. When we worship God, in spirit and in truth, we do not seek help from things; we use things according to their nature, but we seek help from the Supreme alone.

There is no bondage in living according to the law; in brief, there is freedom only in that life that lives absolutely according to the law. A law is but a path to new realms, fairer than we have ever known before. To follow any law in life is to increase the greatness and the worth of life, and to follow all the laws of life is to grow perpetually into the highest good that body, mind and soul can possibly desire. And no one could wish for a greater freedom than this. To use the law is to gain our own; to misuse or ignore the law is to deprive ourselves of our own, and bring disorder, want and pain into life instead. The law never binds nor holds down; the power of all law moves eternally toward the heights, that supreme greatness that is waiting for man; and whoever follows the law will move with that power up unto those same heights.

Give God the glory for what you have and you will receive more. Be grateful for the measure that is coming to you and that measure will increase perpetually. This is the law and it will never fail unless you fail to do to others what God is doing to you. Giving and receiving must be equal in your life. We must give something for everything we receive; nothing is free; the universe is not built in that manner; but giving does not imply the gift of things. True giving and true being are one and the same in real life.

The act of giving produces just as much joy as the act of receiving, because both add to the richness of existence. When we give much we bring forth much from the depths of divine being, and what we bring forth becomes a permanent part of actual life. When we give much we add to life from the within; when we receive much we add to life from the without; and when the richness of the within is harmoniously blended with the richness of the without, then real living begins. But the two must be equal. When we give more than we receive, or receive more than we give, discord follows, and herein we find the cause of many troubles and ills. The lesser without cannot receive the greater within, nor can the greater without be appropriated and appreciated by the lesser within. The small, undeveloped mind cannot enjoy the sublime grandeur of nature, nor can the great, highly developed mind find contentment in crude, uncultivated surroundings. The without and the within must be in harmony if the highest happiness and the truest life is to be enjoyed, and this harmony is invariably secured when giving and receiving are equal. In truth, there is no other way; if we would have the real correspond with the ideal, and the capacity to enjoy be as large as the good things we have found to enjoy, we must give as much as we receive and receive as much as we give.

Before we can receive those things in the without that have worth, we must bring forth worth from the within. What we bring forth from the within we always give to the world, because no person can enrich his own spiritual life without enriching the whole world thereby. Before we can receive the best of all things in the without, we must bring forth the best of all things from the within. But to desire to give to the world from the richness of our own nature is not sufficient; many have done this and have found themselves in want, both physical and spiritual. To desire to receive is just as necessary as to desire to give. The two desires should be equally strong, and together should hourly grow in strength. The desire to receive is just as good as the desire to give, providing the two desires are equally dear to the heart. The more we receive the more we can give, and the more we give the greater our capacity to receive. Therefore, by placing ourselves in that position where we can constantly give more and more and constantly receive more and more, we not only add more and more to the richness and beauty and perfection of our own life, but we become a great power for good in the world. And this is our highest aim.

Before we can live a great life and receive from the external world those things that naturally belong to a great life, we must give forth into real life more and more of our own inherent greatness. Before we can receive as much from the world of things as our largest personal needs and desires may demand, we must unfold, develop and use those powers and talents that are necessary to the building of greater and greater things. Be of great use in the world and you give more and more to the world. In response the world will bring your own to you. He who actively is much, gives much; and he gives the most who serves the best.

To serve the human race in the largest and highest sense, we must bring forth into living expression the truest, the best and the greatest that we can possibly find in the depths of our own sublime being. And to this end we need all the inspiration we can receive from nature, all the love and friendship we can receive from man, and all the wisdom and power we can receive from God.

To become all that we are destined to become, we must receive the largest possible measure from every source, but we cannot receive the largest possible measure from any source unless we give all we have the power to give whenever we have the privilege to do so. And this privilege is ever present. Whatever our field of action may be we may give the very best that there is within us; and we will not do so in vain. Live a great life where you are; hide nothing that has worth; use every talent in full measure; bring forth into life and usefulness the highest powers that you know you possess, and you will enter into a greater and greater life, until you finally reach the supreme heights of exalted spiritual attainments. Awaken everything within you that can, in any manner, enrich, beautify and perfect the whole of life. Do not limit the giving of your greatest self to any one part or any one group of parts. Live for the universe and all that the vastness of the cosmos may contain.

The more we all give to the whole of life the more we all shall receive from the whole of life. We therefore have everything to gain by giving more and more everywhere, and by receiving more and more from every source in order that they may give again in still greater measure. And herein we find the secret to that beautiful life that God has prepared for them that love Him.

"Be not anxious for your life." Live your life according to the very highest light that is within you; use fully and well all the powers that you have received; give your best to the world at all times and under every circumstance, and depend upon the Infinite for everything that existence may need or desire. You will receive it. You need not be anxious about anything. God is greater than anything that can possibly happen. Have faith in Him and He will see you safely through. Things go wrong only when you fail to be your best and fail to take God with you in everything you do. It is therefore in your power to place yourself in that position where everything will go right. The lilies of the field are all that beautiful lilies can possibly be, and they depend wholly upon the powers divine that are within them. Accordingly, they are an inspiration to all the world.

CHAPTER VIII

And All Things Shall Be Added

*But seek ye first his kingdom and his righteousness;
and all these things shall be added unto you.*
—MAT. 6:33.

The kingdom of God is within, and manifests through man as the spiritual life. His righteousness is the right use of all that is contained in the elements of the spiritual life. The spiritual life being the complete life, the full expression of life in body, mind and soul, it is evident that the right use of the spiritual life will produce and bring everything that man may need or desire. The source of everything has the power to produce everything, providing the power within that source is used according to exact spiritual law.

The spiritual life being the source of all that is necessary to a full and perfect life, and the kingdom of God within being the source of the spiritual life, we can readily understand why the kingdom should be sought first; and also, why everything that we may require will be added when the first thought is given to spiritual living and righteous action. Righteous action, however,

53

is not simply moral action, but the right use of the elements of life in all action.

To seek His kingdom first, it is not necessary to withdraw from the world, nor to deny oneself the good things that exist in the world; to seek the kingdom first is to give one's strongest thought to the spiritual life, and to make spiritual thought the predominating thought in everything that one may do in life. In other words, go to God first for everything, place your greatest dependence upon His power to carry you through everything, and live so close to His kingdom within that you are fully conscious of that kingdom every moment.

To seek the kingdom first, the heart must be in the spirit; that is, to live the spiritual life must be the predominating desire; but the mental conception of the spiritual life must not be narrow; in brief, that conception must contain the perfection of everything that can possibly appear in life. To think of the spiritual life as being distinct from mind and body is to deter the spiritual life from being expressed in mind and body; but what is not expressed is not lived. To think about the spiritual, or to feel the emotional power of the spiritual is not sufficient; but that is as far as the spiritual life has been taken by the average person; that the other things were not added is therefore no fault of the law.

The spiritual life must be thoroughly lived in mind and body; the power of the spirit must be made the soul of all power, and the law of spiritual action must be made the rule and guide in all action. When the spiritual is lived in all life, the richness, the quality and the worth of the spiritual will be produced in all life, and spiritual worth is the sum total of all worth.

To enter the kingdom within is to enter health, harmony and happiness, because these three great principles reign supremely in the spiritual life of man. Therefore, by seeking the kingdom, health will be added, harmony will be added, happiness will be added. It is impossible to be sick in the spiritual life; and discord and unhappiness can no more exist in such a life than darkness can exist in the most brilliant light. But to seek the kingdom is not sufficient; we must also seek his righteousness. If we misuse any organ, faculty, function or power anywhere in body, mind or soul, we cannot remain in health no matter how spiritual we may try to be.

To seek his righteousness is to use everything in our world as God uses everything in His world; which means, in harmony with its own nature, in harmony with its sphere of action and in harmony with the law that tends upward and onward forever. Righteous action is that action that is always harmonious and that always works for better things, greater things, higher things.

To enter the kingdom within is to enter more power, because there is no limit to the power of the spirit; and the more power we enter into or become conscious of, the more power we will give to mind and body. In consequence, the more spiritual we become the stronger we become, the more able we become, the more competent we become, and the more we can accomplish whatever our work may be. And he who can do good work in the world invariably receives the good things in the world. To his life will be added all those things that can make personal existence rich and beautiful.

To enter the kingdom is to enter the life of freedom. There is no bondage in the spirit, and as we grow in the spirit we grow out of all bondage; one adverse condition after another disappears until absolute freedom is gained. All bondage comes from incompleteness in living, and misuse of life in doing. But the spiritual life is full and complete, and it follows the law of righteous action in all doing; therefore, when we seek first His kingdom and His righteousness, perfect freedom in all things and at all times will invariably be added.

When we seek first the kingdom, all other things are not added in some mysterious manner; nor do they come of themselves regardless of our conscious effort to work in harmony with the law of life; that is, the law of being and doing all that lies within the power of life. We receive from the kingdom only what we are prepared to use in the living of a great life, and in the doing of great and noble things in the world. We receive only in proportion to what we give; and it is only as we work well that we produce results; but by entering the spiritual life we receive as much as, we may require in order to give as much as we desire; and we gain the power to do everything that is necessary to give worth and superiority to our present state of existence.

When we enter the spiritual life we gain every quality that is required in making life full and complete in our own state of being; and we gain the power to produce and create in the external world whatever we may need or desire. In other words, we receive everything we want from the within, and we gain the power to produce everything we want in the without. We therefore need never take anxious thought about these "other things." By seeking first His kingdom and His righteousness, we shall positively receive them. The way will be opened, and we shall be abundantly supplied with the best that life can give.

Depend upon me. I will provide. This is the Word, eternally spoken from on high; and every awakened soul has learned the message, but the few alone have discerned its real interpretation.

God is rich, and nothing is too good for the children of God. The Spirit of the Infinite will provide; not bare necessities, but everything. Ask what thou wilt and I will answer thee.

It is the will of God that we should seek everything that is good, worthy and beautiful. The life of man should be full and complete; human existence should be rich in body, mind and soul, for this is the great divine purpose.

To think that we must live on bare necessities in order to be spiritual, is to limit our faith in the goodness and the power of God. The kingdom of God is at hand now; we are expected to enter now, and this kingdom is abundantly supplied with everything that can enrich, perfect and beautify human life.

Seek ye first the kingdom, and all other things shall be added; not simply enough to live on, but all things. The love of God is infinite, and we cannot think of infinite love as wanting to give less than all. God has the power to give all. He also has the desire to give all, and therefore every soul may, at any time, receive all that present development can take possession of.

The more we ask of God the more we please God. To give is the highest pleasure of true love, and God is true love. To ask Him for everything, the most of everything and the best of everything is to enter into the life of the highest joy of heaven; and to live in such a life is to live indeed.

When we do not have what we want or what we need, we should remember that Spirit can provide, and that Spirit will provide if we only so desire. Depend upon me. I will not forsake thee nor leave thee. I am thy Redeemer, I will care for thee.

Take God at His word. Have faith in the message that comes from on high. Believe with all the power of mind and soul that

God will do what love will do, because God is love. Open the heart to the influx of infinite love, and all that God can give will come with His love.

Do not hesitate to ask God for material things. God owns the universe. Everything is the product of His creative power; therefore it is all good, and what is good is good for man. What you can use to promote the welfare of everybody, including yourself, you may receive. Only remember this, that things spiritual must come first in your thought. You may have abundances of things material; there is more than enough to provide everybody with all the luxuries of life. You will not deprive anybody of anything by accepting from God all that His love can give. Others may receive as much from the same source; but seek first the things of the spirit, for this is the law.

Consider the lilies of the field. Why should not you be arrayed like one of these? It is the will of God that you should be, and you will give Him great pleasure by asking Him to clothe you even more gorgeously than they. But we must remember that we are not to take these things from others; we are to receive them from God. There is a great difference between the two methods, and there are few in the world that can see it.

To receive from God we must love the spiritual the best, though we must neither despise nor ignore the material. All is from God, and all will minister to the joy and beauty of life when used in harmony with a life that is lived in God. When we live in God, all things will be turned to good account, and when we work with God, all things will work together for greater good.

The world tries to get from man; the perfect way is to receive from God; and the moment we adopt the latter method, the way will be opened. Spirit will lead; we will know at each step what we are to do, and what step to take next will always be clear. Live close to God and have faith; no matter what may come or not, depend upon the spirit to lead and provide, and you will always do what is best.

However, we must never think that it is best for anyone to live in poverty, trouble and pain; no, this is never best, not even for a moment. The Infinite can provide something better here and now, and it is His will and good pleasure to do so.

When days of darkness are at hand, cling to the great truth, spirit will provide. Think of it constantly; live in the very soul of its presence; believe in it from the very depths of the heart. Things will take a turn. The door of opportunity will open. The desired change will come. There is nothing in the world that the Spirit cannot change for the better; therefore we may with perfect faith ask for any change desired. The best is intended for all of us. God is ever ready to give everything. Ask what thou wilt and I will answer thee.

> To think of thee and feel thy presence near,
> To rise above the world of doubt and fear,
> To enter where the many mansions be,
> To hold communion face to face with thee.
>
> To find the secret place where all is still,
> To feel thy joy and life my being thrill,
> To know that health and wholeness now are mine,
> To see thy light within forever shine,
>
> To feel the peace that passeth thought and speech,
> To know that I the endless heights shall reach,
> That I thy Son for evermore shall be,
> These are the sweetest thoughts of life to me.

CHAPTER IX

When Life Is Worth Living

To establish permanently the living of life in the spiritual state of being is the greatest need of man. But this is not possible so long as we live in that conception of spirituality that forgets the body. The body is the temple of the spirit, and must therefore receive just as much thought and attention as we give to the spirit. To neglect the body is to make real spirituality impossible, because real spirituality is a living thing, and must have a highly developed personality through which this living may be expressed. Spirituality is not simply in thought, feeling or abstract contemplation; there is no spirituality without the actual coming forth of real soul life; but the life of the soul does not come forth into tangible personal living unless the body is trained to respond to that life.

The spirituality that we seek is that full expression of the soul that fills every atom in the body and gives the sublime wholeness of divinity to the entire being of man. To be spiritual is to be complete in body, mind and soul; to live the fullness of real life in every element of life, and to bring forth the truest, the best and the most beautiful that exists within us. To become spiritual is to refine everything, perfect everything, beautify everything, and make the ideal real, not only in thought but in every part of physical life, mental life and spiritual life. To grow in spirituality is to continue perpetually to spiritualize the body, as well as mind and soul, until the visible man is as pure, as strong, as wholesome and as beautiful as the highest state of divine existence.

True spirituality will give health and vigor to the body, power and brilliancy to the mind, strength and perfection to the character, and sublime loveliness to the soul. The more spiritual you become the more beautiful you become in person, the more refined you become in all the elements of your nature, the more powerful you become in every thought and action, and the more comfort, happiness and real satisfaction you will receive from everything you may do in life. When spirituality is highly developed you live constantly on the heights; you see all things as they are in the real; you know that you are created in the image and likeness of God; you are in constant touch with the beauty and splendor of the cosmic world, and your joy is supreme. You are living in the light of the spirit, and your mind at times is so illumined by that light that your understanding of higher wisdom becomes extraordinary. You thus enter those lofty realms from which all true prophets have received their inspiration, and, accordingly, you become one of those who are chosen to be taught of God.

To enter real spirituality is to anchor the mind in that very power that holds and guides the universe; and such a mind is always safe. Such a mind will not go wrong; and even though it be strongly tempted, it will be removed from danger before it is too late. There is something in the higher world about us that can and does protect the soul; and those who are fixed on high in the spirit are ever in the care of this divine protection. Dangers, calamities or catastrophes will never touch them; they are invariably taken out safely, no matter what may happen; they are ever in the hands of God, and all is always well.

This higher guiding power, however, does not simply protect the chosen ones from that which is not desired; but those who have supreme faith in the spirit will be led on and on into the larger and larger realization of that which is desired. The spirit contains all, and to grow in the spirit is to receive all. Not simply that all that satisfies the demands of the intellect or the feelings of the soul, but that all that fully supplies every want, desire or need of the whole man. Spirituality is the highest good of all life realized in full living expression. In the spiritual life there is no need, neither is there any false desire. Every desire is true to the great purpose of eternal life, and every desire is fulfilled. In spiritual life every prayer is inspired by the wisdom of the spirit, and such prayers are always answered. Whatever God may lead us to do he will always give us the power to do.

The spiritual state of being is the great foundation of all being, and the source of everything that comes forth into perfect being; therefore, the more deeply we enter into the life and the power of the spirit the more fully conscious we become of those greater things that real life has in store; and whatever we become conscious of we invariably bring forth into tangible existence. The spiritual life contains real life, real power, real wisdom, real love, real harmony, real health, real purity, real peace, real joy, and to develop spirituality is to realize more and more of the real of these things until the perfection of divine being is unfolded and lived in the present personal form. In consequence, when we are in the spiritual life we need sacrifice nothing that has real value, while we gain more and more of everything that has greater value. When we begin to live the spiritual life we begin to feel that we are now upon the solid rock of eternal being, and we feel absolutely secure. We realize that we are in safety, in divinity, in the protecting care of higher power. We are becoming more and more conscious of the cosmic atmosphere, and this gives added assurance of complete protection, because this higher, sublimated atmosphere is so surcharged with living spirit that no ill from the world can possibly pass through. We are absolutely out of the ills of the world when we are in the spirit, just as we are absolutely out of darkness when we are in the light. And to grow in the spirit the first essential is to take what spiritual life we can now understand and give that life full, living expression in every atom of body, soul and mind.

There can be no real spirituality developed so long as we try to make such developments a matter of the soul alone; mind and body must be included or our efforts simply result in feelings and sentiments that are neither wholesome nor harmless. Spirituality is not a matter of sentiment, nor is it wholly concerned with a future state of existence. Spirituality is a full life just for today. It is a life that is all that it is now, and those who are in the spirit know that the time that now is, is eternal.

One touch of the spirit and all is well. Darkness and pain will vanish, sickness and sorrow take flight; weakness and bondage will pass away, and troubles can exist no more. To be touched by the spirit is to be filled through and through with the spirit, and where the spirit is there evil is not. What we have seen in our visions shall come to remain. What is revealed from on high shall come and abide with us always. Therefore let the soul dream on. Disturb not the peace of those sweet celestial slumbers, for what to us may appear to be spiritual sleep is but life in a greater world. And thus something from above comes to tell us, "Dream on, fair soul, dream on."

To worship God in spirit and in truth is to so live that we can always feel that he is with us no matter what we may think or say or do. To worship God is to take Him with us in everything, ask Him for everything, have faith that He will give us everything, and be grateful to Him because we inwardly know that we are receiving everything. To worship is not to believe and adore, but to live and love; not simply to accept the truth but to make the truth the living soul of every thought and word and deed. When we worship God in truth, we enter into His presence knowing that He is divine perfection and that we are created in His image and likeness. To believe that we are depraved beings, base sinners or imperfect human creatures, is not to be in the truth, because to be in the truth we are as God is. Therefore, while we have those beliefs we cannot worship God in truth. To worship God in truth we must enter the truth, and to enter the truth is to know that man is even now the perfect image of the Most High.

To worship God in the spirit, is to forget the letter and enter into the spiritual realization of His omnipresent life. When we are in the spirit we do not worship with audible words or visible attitudes, but with that exalted spiritual feeling that enters into the very soul of the Infinite and there awakens to the great eternal truth that "My Father and I are one." When we are in the spirit we inwardly know that "God is closer than breathing, nearer than hands and feet," and we can feel that sublime nearness thrill every atom in our being. We need nothing to prove to us that we are one with God, for we can feel that it is the truth. Nor do we question any more whether God be personal or not. We know that we are with Him and that He is with us; and that is sufficient. His personal presence is more real to us than our own existence; we therefore need not reason on that subject. We have seen Him in the spirit, but that which is, in the spirit, form cannot measure, nor words define.

The word of God is the word of truth. All truth is Scripture wherever found or by whom presented; and all Scripture is written when the mind is in the spirit. Therefore, to understand the Scripture we must enter the spirit, and read while illumined by the spirit. We shall then find, upon every page, "the bread of heaven," "the waters of life," "the meat that ye know not of." The key to the Scriptures is not some system of symbolical interpretation, nor some special method of metaphysical or spiritual analysis. The key is simply to enter the spirit when you begin to read. The spirit reveals everything that is sacred and true.

To live exclusively in materiality, that is, in the lower story of being, is the cause of all weakness and weariness. The remedy for such conditions will therefore be found in spirituality, which means to live in the upper story. So long as the mind is "high" in the world of consciousness there can be no weakness or weariness in the person. We cannot be weary while we are filled with the strength of the Most High, and we are in perfect touch with this great strength while the mind is living in the "high places" of the spirit. When we come down to the earth, we lose this superior power and become weak as mere men; we are limited in every respect and have to watch ourselves at every turn lest we overtax the system. But when we do all things in the realization that we are spiritual beings filled with supreme power from on high, there is no limit to what we can do. Our strength

66

is eternally renewed because we are waiting upon the Lord; we are living with Him, doing all things for Him, and in return we receive all things from Him.

When the mind lives constantly in the higher states of being, more perfect oneness with the Infinite is attained. We come nearer and nearer to the Life and the Spirit of the Supreme, and, in consequence, we are supplied with new life and power every moment. We are going into the source of all power; we are beginning to live and move and have our being in the very essence of that power, and we are becoming stronger by far than all the weakness and the weariness in the world. We are no longer subject to the laws of material existence; what holds true in the life of mere man does not hold true for us any more; we have entered a new life and are ascending triumphantly to the supreme heights of that life. The seeming weakness of the flesh has given place to the limitless strength of the Spirit; for the very moment we begin to live in the spirit, the power of the spirit begins to live in us, and that which lives in us lives in every element of the body as well as in every attribute of mind and soul.

Spirituality is the perfect remedy for all the ills of life, and to live the spiritual life is the greatest thing that man can do. Therefore, to promote spiritual growth among all minds that are ready is of more importance than all other objects and aims combined. Thousands realize this, and, in consequence, are ever in search for methods through which the life of the spirit may be found. Methods, however, are of secondary importance. When the heart begins to feel the need of the spirit, and all the powers of mind begin to desire the spirit, the perfect way will be opened. To promote spiritual growth we must live in the spiritual center of the divine that is within us, but that divine center is not found through methods. No system of mental gymnastics can open the gates to the kingdom within; nor can any system of logical reasoning in abstract truth cause the mind to be illumined with light from on high. Spiritual illumination does not come through a mere intellectual process, however exact; it comes only when the desires of the heart are spiritualized by a power that is infinitely greater than man.

To think the truth, even with absolute exactness, will not avail unless we think in the spirit of truth. The intellectual form of the truth has no power; it is the inner spirit of the truth that gives life, freedom and illumination to man. And when we begin to know this inner spirit of the truth our minds have entered into the very soul of the real. Then it is that we gain power that to many seems superhuman; then it is that we take full possession of our own life and our own destiny; then it is that we find the faith that moves mountains, and through the life of this faith we press on and on to the great goal we have in view, removing every barrier in the way, overcoming every difficulty, surmounting every obstacle, rising higher than ever before every time we fall, transforming every seeming defeat into a great and glorious victory, passing through the fires of tribulation without even a hair being scorched, and coming out of every trying experience with greater purity and greater strength, realizing one ideal after another, ascending from one pinnacle of attainment to one that is higher still, finding answer after answer to the prayers we prayed in days gone by, until every desire is fulfilled and every dream of the soul made true.

There is no reason whatever why anyone should become discouraged, or be tempted to give up because the good things desired are not realized when expected. That which is your own will positively come to you, and everything is your own that you can use in the building of a greater and more beautiful life. Continue in the faith that you will now begin to realize the fullness of life, and enter into the inner spirit of that faith. Some of the greatest things in the world have been gained after many years of constant faith and prayer—things that would not have been gained if those who prayed had lived in discouragement and doubt. If there is anything that you can use in the building of a great life, pray for it until you receive it no matter how many months or years may be required to cause your prayer to come true. Pray in the inner spirit of faith and when the time is ripe, be it tomorrow or twenty years from now, your prayer will be answered.

When your prayers are not answered at once, do not come to the conclusion that it is not best for you to have it; if that which you pray for will add to the welfare of somebody's life, it is best for you to have it. Therefore, continue to pray for it until you receive it. It is best that you should have everything that is good and true and beautiful. All that is good is good for man, and it is the will of God that man should receive it. But God gives us only that which we desire. We have individual choice, and we must express our desire in the true spirit of faith. What we ask for will come when our faith is right and our life prepared to properly use the great good desired.

To promote spiritual growth the inner light must shine in the outer life, and the inner world of divine truth must be expressed in every part of mind and body. The expression of the divinity within is absolutely necessary, and must be in every direction. Thousands today are expressing truth only for the purpose of securing health of body and peace of mind, and though they are having good results they will find ere long that in trying to perfect only a part of the outer life they have failed to bring forth the whole of the inner life. They will also find that the marvelous powers of the within have been permitted to sleep. After some years such minds will find that they have accomplished nothing more than being well and comfortable physically. But this is not all that we are living for. A genius is asleep in the subconscious of every mind; a spiritual giant is within us awaiting recognition; and in the soul is the Christ knocking at the door. These must not be kept waiting age after age while we are only concerned with being well and happy on the surface. It is not right to live a small life no matter how comfortable that life may be when we have received the gifts of the supreme life from on high.

The expression of the spirit should be universal in all the actions of man. The labor of the hands should be filled with the life of the spirit; the work of the mind should be animated with the one power of spirit, and every act of consciousness should feel the divine presence of the spirit. There are few, however, who think of expressing divine spirit in every day's work, and consequently, the spiritual life becomes a thing apart. But when the personal life is separated from the spirit, darkness, confusion, sickness and trouble begin; existence becomes a burden, and though we may possess the wealth of the world, life has nothing of worth to give. There is no joy in things unless the power of the spirit is in the world of things. There is nothing to live for unless we live for the spirit, and when we begin to live for the spirit all things, from the least importance in the physical realm to the most precious elements in the highest spiritual realms— all become ministering angels, adding eternally to the worth, the beauty and the joy of personal life. To him who lives in the spirit, everything in life has much to give, and to him, the best alone is given.

When we think, the mind should be filled with the spirit, and our intellects will become brilliant in the true sense of that term. When we read, our eyes should be filled with the spirit, and our sight will ever become stronger and better. When we work, every muscle in the body should be filled with the spirit, and we should renew our strength from the source divine. We thus cause the outer life and the inner life to become one life, and it is such a life that we are here to live now. Say that life is beautiful, no matter how things may appear on the surface. Say that you are strong and well no matter how the body may feel. You will thus speak the truth about the true state of being; and what you say, you create. Say that you are well and you create health. Say that life is divinely beautiful and you create such a life. And what we create today, we shall realize tomorrow.

There are a number of methods through which the spiritual nature of man can be developed and brought into larger and larger expression, but the majority of those methods are so complex that they lead more into intellectuality than into spirituality. To develop the mind, with its many faculties, complex methods are, as a rule, necessary, but to develop the soul, the simpler the methods are, the better. The secret is to keep the eye single upon the sublime spiritual state, to form the highest possible conception of the most perfect spiritual qualities imaginable, and to think of those things. The power of concentration is truly extraordinary whenever it may be applied, and its effectiveness is nowhere as thorough as in the world of the spirit. To think constantly of things spiritual, with an effort to enter more and more into the real life of the spirit, is to spiritualize all the elements of thought, all the phases of consciousness, and all the active states of realization. In consequence, everything in human life will become more spiritual.

What we think of we create; therefore the more we think of things spiritual the more spirituality we shall develop; and when the whole of thought is concentrated constantly upon our highest spiritual ideal, we shall actually move into the real spiritual state. There is a spiritual state of consciousness immediately above the usual conscious state, and it is the lifting of mind and thought up into this higher state that produces spirituality; therefore, spiritual development will necessarily require the ascending tendency in every action in life. This requirement, however, is invariably supplied, when the power of attention is constantly directed upon the spiritual state. When we think of that which is spiritual, everything in life begins to ascend towards the higher spiritual states; that is, when our thinking of the spiritual is inspired with a deep soul desire to rise and live on the heights.

Live with the beautiful side in human nature and your own life will grow more and more beautiful until you become an inspiration to all the world. Look for the greater good in all things and you will find God in all things. And when you find God in all things God will be with you in all things.

Say that life is beautiful, no matter how things may appear on the surface. Say that you are strong and well no matter how the body may feel. You will thus speak the truth about the true state of being; and what you say, you create. Say that you are well and you create health. Say that life is divinely beautiful and you create such a life. And what we create today, we shall realize tomorrow.

The pure in heart shall see God, and to be pure in heart is to think pure thoughts, the thought of sublime spiritual truth. The reason we do not see God is found in the fact that we have clouded our minds with impure thoughts, thought that is out of harmony with the divine order of things. Pure water is transparent; the same is true of a pure mind. The deep things of God are easily discerned through a pure mind, just as easily as the rocks of the river bed when the water is pure and still.

CHAPTER X

The Way, the Truth and the Life

Jesus saith unto him, I am the way, and
the truth, and the life; no one
cometh unto the Father but by me.
—JOHN 14:6.

The great statements of Jesus Christ were never spoken from the personal, but always from the impersonal. No truth ever sprung from the personal mind because it is only the impersonal that can touch the universal, and it is only in the universal that absolute truth can be found. When the mind enters the impersonal state, consciousness comes in touch with the cosmic state of being, and in that state we realize the "I Am" of being. We discern what the "I Am" actually is, and we find that the consciousness of the "I Am" is the open door to the limitless vastness of the spiritual universe. "I am the door." Enter through the door of "I Am" and we pass into that immense world that is found on the upper side, or the divine side of sublime existence.

The "I Am" in every soul is the spirit of Christ within us, and when we become conscious of the Christ within us we can truthfully say that "the mind that was in Christ Jesus, the same mind is in me." The mind that was in Christ Jesus knew the "I Am" of eternal being; in brief, was the "I Am" of eternal being, and therefore could say that I am the way, and the truth, and the life. But this same "I Am" is in every soul and constitutes the real "me" of every soul, and as we grow in Christ we grow into the realization of that great truth that we are one with Christ and that the same Christ that reigned supremely in the personality of Jesus shall reign supremely in us.

The Christ within us is the only begotten of the Father, and is created in the image and likeness of the Father. There is only one Son of God, but this one Son reigns in every soul, and constitutes the "I Am" in every soul. The "I Am" that occupies the throne of your spiritual being is the only begotten Son of God, and as this Son is like the Father you cannot grow into the likeness of the Father unless you do so through the Son. Nor can you enter into the presence of the Father without going through the Son, because it is the Son that unites the Father with you.

The Son of God is one with God; therefore if you wish to realize your oneness with God you must enter into the life and the spirit of the Son. In other words, you must become conscious of the "I Am" within you because it is this "I Am" that is created in the image of God, and we are not one with God unless we realize that we are created in the image of God. To be one with God is to know that we are in the Father and the Father in us, but we cannot enter into that consciousness wherein we know that we are in the Father until we are conscious of our exact likeness to the Father.

When Jesus declared, I am the way, he spoke in the consciousness of the Christ. It was the supreme "I Am" that made this great statement, and this "I Am" is the way. The supreme "I Am" is the way to everything that man may need or desire throughout eternity, for "I Am" in God, and in God we find the allness of all that is. The "I Am" is the way to God, because it is the "I Am" in man that is always one with God. "I am the door," and there is no other door; it is therefore evident that no one cometh unto the Father but by me.

To go to God you must go by way of the Christ; that is, you must enter into the inner consciousness of the Christ that reigns within us; you must enter so deeply into the spirit of your own sublime being that you can readily realize that "I Am," and know that "I Am" is not distinct from you but is the real and the eternal of you. "Where I am there ye shall be also." You shall some day enter that same exalted state where your consciousness of the "I Am" will be so perfect that you will know that you are "I Am." Then the supreme "I Am" will speak in you as he did in Jesus and will in like manner declare in you, "I am the way."

When we find the spirit of Christ within us we find the way; we then enter the path, the path that leads to the fullness of life and the perfection of being. To daily ascend higher and higher in the consciousness of this spirit of the Christ is to follow the Christ, and to follow the Christ is to enter the Kingdom.

The "I Am" is the truth because all truth has its source in the divine being of man. That the real man is created in the image of God is the one supreme truth, and the real man is the "I Am." To know the truth is to enter into the life and the spirit of the "I Am" within; that is, the Christ within, and to enter into the Christ is to enter into freedom because there can be no bondage or ill whatever in Him. This is how we gain freedom when we know the truth; not by forming intellectual concepts about truth, but by entering consciously into the spirit of the Christ within which is the truth.

To enter into the Christ consciousness is to become conscious of the real being of the Christ, and the real being of the Christ is identical with the real being of man. To become conscious of the real being of man is to know the truth concerning man, and when we know this truth we know that man is divine because man, in his eternal nature, is identical with the nature of the Christ. When we know that we are created in the likeness of truth we know that we are truth, and we can say, when speaking from the Christ consciousness, into which we have entered, "I am the truth." And when we know that we are truth we are conscious only of that which is truth. We cannot be out of the truth when we are in truth, and as there can be no ill or bondage in the truth we must necessarily be in absolute freedom while we are consciously in the truth.

The "I Am" is the life; all life comes from God, and "the life that is in us is the life of the only begotten of God. The life eternal is the life of God in us, and it is the "I Am" in us that lives the life of God in us. To gain the life more abundant it is therefore necessary to enter more and more deeply into the consciousness of the "I Am" within. In brief, the more fully we realize the "I Am" or the Christ within us the more we live, and when we enter so perfectly into the Christ consciousness that we actually know that the real in us is identical with the "I Am" in us, then we begin to live the life eternal; then we actually enter eternity while still in personal form; then we know with positive conviction that we are immortal, and we need no further evidence from any other source whatever.

When we learn that "I am the door" and seek this door in the spiritual life within us, we shall find it; and as we pass through this door we enter the other side of life, the divine side, the eternal side. There we find the kingdom of God that is within us, and beyond is the shining shore. But we are not required to leave the personal form and the physical life in order to live on the other side of life. True being is to live on the spiritual side of life and to manifest the perfection of spiritual being in the personal side of life. Thus the Word becomes flesh and the glory of God is made visible in man.

For narrow is the gate, and straightened the way, that leadeth unto life. And those alone who are in the spirit can find it. Follow the light of the spirit in all things, choose the living Christ as the pattern in all things, and depend upon God in all things. Do not seek the truth; seek the spirit of truth. The spirit leads into all truth. To know the truth is to know the way. To be guided by the spirit into all truth is to walk in the light of the spirit all the way, and the way of light leads into the kingdom of eternal life. Follow the words of the Christ until the spirit is found; then follow the spirit into the greater life of the Christ. Keep the eye single upon that light that is revealed through the spiritual vision of the soul. Where that light is shining there is the gate; beyond is the way that leadeth unto life, and all who are in the spirit shall find it even now.

CHAPTER XI

To Know and Think the Truth

To mentally live in the spiritual understanding of truth and to give constant expression, in thought to the words of truth is to train the mind to know the truth in a larger and larger measure; and to know the truth is to create and express true conditions throughout the entire personality.

A statement of truth is the absolute truth expressed in words; that is, the mental or verbal expression of a certain state of perfect and divine being. Therefore, a statement of truth does not describe things as they are in the external, but describes man as he is in the spirit; and when the mind begins to think of man as he is in the spirit, the perfect qualities of the spirit will be unfolded and brought out into the personal life.

The life of the spirit is the true life of man because man is a spiritual being; the soul is the real man; the mind and the body are merely instruments. For this reason it is evident that when man thinks of himself he must necessarily think of himself as he is in the spirit. The conditions of the body do not describe the divine state of the soul; the soul is real, absolute, divine, perfect, complete, created in the image of God, while the personality is but a partial expression of the real, in many respects incomplete and in a state of development.

When man thinks that the incomplete conditions of his personality constitute himself he is not thinking the truth about himself; his thought is false, and false thinking produces false or detrimental conditions in mind and body.

However, when he thinks of himself as he is in the divine perfection of his being, he is thinking the truth about himself; his thought is the truth and the thinking of truth produces true or wholesome conditions in mind and body. Therefore, so long as man thinks of himself as being an imperfect personality he will cause his personality to be imperfect, weak, sickly and more or less in disorder; but when he constantly thinks of himself as he is in the perfect, wholesome, divine state of his real spiritual being, he will cause his personality to be wholesome, healthful, harmonious and in the most perfect state of order.

The truth gives freedom. To know the truth is to live in the perfect world of truth. When the mind discerns truth, all thought is created in the likeness of truth; all thought is truth; and man is as he thinks. To think the truth is to create that which is true, and when the true comes into being the false ceases to be.

There can be no darkness in the light; there can be no false conditions in the truth; therefore, when man is in the truth, the wholeness and the perfection of the truth will pervade his entire being through and through. Every part will be true to the truth, and every element will express the divinity of man.

When the mind thinks the truth, every mental conception of true being will formulate itself in a statement of truth; these statements will convey to man's intelligence the higher understanding of all that is. The mind will learn to see all things as they are in truth; the divine perfection of all things will be realized; all thought will contain the spirit of truth, and man himself will be the truth in every fibre of his being. Therefore, every mind should think statements of truth as frequently as possible, and with the deepest conviction possible.

The conditions of the personality are the direct effects of the states of the mind; therefore, the conditions of the personality will always be true, good and perfect so long as the states of the mind are true; and the states of the mind will always be true so long as the mind thinks the truth-thinks the truth about man as he is in the divine perfection of his real spiritual being.

To train the mind to think the real truth about man, statements of truth of every possible description should be employed extensively. In brief, the mind should be daily drilled in the thinking of absolute truth; that is, the mental or verbal expression of statements of truth; and to enter into the spiritual understanding of the real significance of every statement should be the central purpose in view.

The mere mechanical repetition of such statements will not avail; the real truth of each statement is discerned only when the mind enters into the very soul of the statement; and it is the real truth that we wish to know, because it is the knowing of real truth that alone makes for freedom in life and that produces the fullness of life. To train the mind to think the real truth, the following statements of truth may be employed, though the wording may be changed to correspond with the state of each individual need or the degree of conscious development in the spiritual life.

The perfection of my being is now realized in the spiritual understanding of truth.

The understanding of truth reveals to the mind the divine perfection of all being, and the more spiritual this understanding is, the more clearly can the divinity of man be discerned. Spirituality illumines, because to be spiritual is to live in the supreme light of the spirit. In the spirit there is no darkness; therefore, in the spirit all things can be seen as they are, and to see all things as they are is to see that all things are created in the likeness of God. The realization of the great truth that being is perfect, created in the image of God, will cause this perfection to be expressed. What we realize in the spirit will be expressed in the person. Therefore, when the real truth of this statement is understood, the personal life will be a manifestation of the spiritual life, and all will be well in body, mind and soul.

God is love, and in Him I live and move and have my being.

To live the true spiritual life, the life of complete emancipation and high spiritual attainment, it is necessary to love all things with the pure, limitless love of the soul, but such a love cannot be realized so long as consciousness is personal only. It is when we feel that we live in the love of God that we gain consciousness of that love that loves all things at all times, and we shall invariably feel that we do live in the love of God when we know the real truth of the statement that God is boundless love and that we have our being in Him. To realize that we live in God is to feel His presence, and when we do feel His presence we become absolutely filled with a love that is so tender, so beautiful, so high and so sublime, that we are placed completely at one with all the universe. We immediately transcend, and eliminate entirely, every adverse feeling; we are at peace with everything and that peace is animated with the spirit of that love that cannot be measured. To live in such a love is supreme joy, and it is the privilege of every soul now.

I am fixed on high in the spirit of truth.

The I Am of every soul can truthfully make this statement, for real being is permanently established in the true life of the spirit, and as every individual is the I Am of his own being, every individual, to speak the truth, must make this statement about himself. To realize the truth of this statement is to enter more and more into the fixed state of true being, and to grow in the realization of this state is to gain that absolute safety and security where the soul finds complete divine protection. To be in the spirit of truth is to be in the very life of true existence, and to be fixed in this life is to occupy a permanent place in God's own beautiful world. In other words, to be fixed in the spirit of truth is to be anchored in God, and we can readily realize how absolutely secure such a state of being must be. When we make this statement we should try to realize what existence in the truth must necessarily mean, how it must feel to be in the consciousness of the spirit of such an existence, and what a life must hold in store that is permanently established on the very heights of that existence. The more fully we enter into the soul of the truth that this statement conveys, the sooner we shall realize the truth itself; and when we do, we shall know that we are fixed on high, permanently established in the spirit of truth, forever anchored in God.

My spiritual being is the expression of eternal life.

The life eternal is the whole of real, absolute, limitless life, and the real, spiritual man is this life individualized and expressed. The life eternal contains the whole complete existence; therefore, to live the life eternal is to live all that there is in absolute existence. It is the life eternal that the soul lives; and since man is the soul, he should affirm that he is living the life eternal now and that his true being is the perfect expression of that life. The life eternal is the life of the divinity that is in man, and the true being of man constitutes that divinity; but we manifest in personal life only that which we become conscious of; therefore the mind must be unfolded to realize the true nature of the life eternal before we can enter into life now. To unfold the mind into this conscious realization, all thinking should be animated with the highest spiritual conception of the life eternal that we can possibly form, and the great truth that the true spiritual being of man is the perfect expression of that life should be held before the mental vision constantly. In addition, every effort we make to live the life, that is, to live in the soul of real life, will cause this statement, not only to seem true in the ideal, but to prove itself to be true in the actual.

I am ever ascending into the greater and greater freedom of God.

God is absolute freedom, and man is eternally becoming what God is. To realize this truth is to place life in that position where personal existence will, at every step in human advancement, be in full possession of that measure of freedom that present consciousness can possibly involve. This means that the life of every moment will be absolutely free and that the measure of freedom will increase in perfect harmony with the increase of the mind's capacity for freedom. The real man is ever in possession of all the freedom that present development can comprehend and employ, and is ever ascending into the greater freedom of God; therefore, to enter into the realization of this truth is to keep the eye upon the supreme freedom, to steadily rise into more and more of that freedom, and this is the true path to complete emancipation. When we steadily grow into the freedom of God, we must necessarily grow out of everything that is limited, undesirable or adverse. The lesser passes away as we pass upward and onward into the ever expanding world of the greater.

God is health and wholeness, and I am his image and likeness.

There can be no sickness in God; for the same reason there can be no sickness in the real being of man; and as each individual is what he is in his own real being, he must necessarily be well at all times. The real man cannot possibly be sick any more than light can be darkness, because he is as God is; therefore no man can truthfully say, at any time, that he is sick, weak or disabled. He cannot be any of these things, no matter what personal conditions may seem to be. The real man is always well, and I am the real man. I am not the body, nor the instrument, nor the garment. I am the I Am, the image of God, the exact likeness of the Most High. When adverse conditions appear in the personality, there are personal causes, either physical or mental, but these conditions can never enter the life of the real spiritual man. The real man continues to be well and strong at all times, and the life of the real man is perpetually a life of perfect health and wholeness. To live constantly in the conscious realization of the life of the real man is to always feel well, in body, mind and soul. There can be no sickness in the body so long as we live in the life of health, and we do live in the life of health so long as we continue in the realization of the great truth that God is health, and that we are as He is. Those adverse conditions that may exist in the body now will entirely disappear the moment we enter into the realization of real life, and begin to live in the spirit of the truth that we are as God is -- perfect and whole, now and forever.

My Father and I are one.

The mind that was in Christ Jesus, the same mind is in you, and this mind knows that My Father and I are One. When we enter into the spirit of the divine mind we realize that there is no separation whatever in the spirit. The spirit of the human soul is absolutely one with the spirit of the Infinite. There is no difference whatever in divine essence or soul life; only the Infinite is God while the human soul is an expression of God, the son of God, the only begotten of God.

When we enter into the very presence of God, we know that no separation can exist in the spirit, and we also learn that the Christ consciousness implies the highest consciousness of this divine oneness. The mind that was in Christ Jesus is conscious of the spiritual oneness that exists between God and man, and we enter into that mind whenever we feel that we are in the presence of God.

To realize that we are one with God in spirit and in truth is to realize that we are also one with the life, the divinity and the perfection of God; and therefore we are as God is; what is in

God is in us; we live the same life that He lives, and since there can be no imperfection in His life, there can be no imperfection in our life.

The spiritual life of man is perfect, and when man enters fully into the consciousness of his spiritual life, his personal life will become the exact expression of His spiritual life. Then the Word will become flesh, and no ill can exist in the body any more. Nor can the untruth any longer exist in the mind.

To grow in the Christ consciousness is to grow in the consciousness of the spiritual life, and as the light of the spiritual life becomes stronger and stronger in mind, these elements of darkness, sickness, adverseness or imperfection that may remain in personal existence will entirely disappear. Then we shall realize the emancipated life, the freedom that comes from the knowing of the truth.

God is my strength. I am strong with His limitless life and power.

To dwell perpetually in the conviction that the strength of the Infinite is our strength is to steadily grow in the conscious realization of power, and the more power we become conscious of the more power we possess. To think of weakness in any sense of the term becomes impossible when we know that the limitless power of the Infinite is just as much ours as it is His. All that the Father hath is mine. And when we cease to think of weakness we shall never again be conscious of weakness.

To think of truth we can never admit that we are weak; we cannot even admit that it is possible for us to become weak. When we feel weak we are simply permitting ourselves to be untrue to ourselves; we ignore the reality of our own being and cause the mind to create conditions in our system that are false. Thus evil begins. But so long as we cause the mind to be fixed in that great truth that God is our strength, we shall not be conscious of anything that is not strength; nor will the mind create any condition that is not true to the truth.

When we realize that the strength of the Infinite is our strength and that the strength of the Infinite is limitless, we must come to the conclusion that we are capable of doing anything that the living of a great life may demand. Whatever we are called upon to do, we are equal to it, because, have we not the power of the Supreme with which to work?

In the light of this truth we can never say that we are unable to do what the hour may require; nor can we say truthfully that we are ever tired, wearied or overcome. Such thoughts do not belong to the truth. While we are in the truth there is nothing that can make us tired; nor is there anything that is too much for us. God is our strength and the power of Him that is within us is greater than anything in the world.

Though the flesh may seem to be weak, it seems so only because we have not fully accepted what is truly our own, the strength of the Infinite. But when we do accept this strength, the power of the spirit will manifest in the flesh; we shall then be strong, through and through, with power from on high. Every part of body, mind and soul will live with limitless life, because God lives with limitless life, and all that the Father hath is mine.

My being is sustained in the Word of Truth.

The word of truth is the coming forth of truth into life; it is truth taking shape and form in the world of being, and to be sustained in the word of truth is to so live that everything in life is shaped, formed and determined by the power of truth.

To think frequently of the great statement that we are sustained in the shaping and forming power of truth is to place the mind more and more perfectly in harmony with that power; in consequence, the mind will be shaped more and more in the exact likeness of truth.

When the mind assumes the form of truth, every action of the mind becomes an expression of truth; the mind itself becomes a true mind and all thinking will convey the elements of truth to every part of the being of man. When the mind is formed by the truth, only true conditions will be formed by the mind; and therefore, neither sickness, inharmony, weakness, adversity, pain nor want can possibly exist anywhere in the human system.

To feel that we are sustained in the word of truth is to produce that deep realization of the power of truth that is so conducive to the full understanding of truth; and as we grow in the understanding of truth we grow into the freedom that is produced by the truth.

The word of truth is the living truth; that is, the power of truth expressed in tangible action; and is therefore distinct from abstract truth, or the mere intellectual conception of truth. The intellectual aspect of truth does not sustain the true life because it has not become the word, or the power of true formation. But the realization of the word of truth takes life into what may be termed truth in action; and when we are in the truth in action we are acting in the truth.

To act, live or think in the truth is to give the sustaining power of truth to every action, and thus every action will not only be a true action, but it will contain the limitless power of truth. This is why no true action can fail, and also why no ill can possibly come to any human personality that lives in the word of truth and that is consciously resolved into the pure spiritual essence of truth.

When the human system is sustained in the word of truth, every part of the system is fixed on high; that is, placed within that true state of being where everything is created in the image of God and where everything is always well. In this state the good alone exists; everything has freedom because it is in the world of absolute freedom, and therefore everything will do what divine purpose planned that it should do. This is the true meaning of freedom, and it is such freedom alone that can give to every soul what the largest life and the greatest joy may need or desire.

"But let your speech be yea, yea; nay, nay." Every statement we make should either affirm that which is true or deny that which is not true. Statements that contain both the elements of truth and the elements of untruth are of the evil one; they confuse the mind and lead to sin, sickness and death. Make no compromise with the untruth, and let no half-truth find expression in your life. Give positive expression, in thought, word, action and life, to that which you know to be real, and eliminate completely what you know to be unreal. Make your life a living affirmation of the great things that are before, and so live that everything you do will deny the lesser things that are passing away.

Spiritual consciousness is in the light of the truth, and can always see the truth clearly. To see the truth clearly is to know the truth, and to know the truth is to be free.

The spiritual understanding of truth is the direct consequence of the mind's insight into that realm where everything is what it is; where nothing can be added and nothing taken away.

When you inwardly feel what you say, you give spiritual power to your words; and what you say will surely come to pass.

CHAPTER XII

Finding the Lost Word

Illumined minds in every age have declared their belief in what may be termed the sacred word; or that formulated statement of truth through which unbounded power could be expressed. According to this belief, anyone who knew this secret word or statement could, by the use of that word, secure anything he might desire. Through this word the sick could be healed, adversity overcome, calamities prevented, enemies turned into friends, earnest desires realized, life prolonged, and everything gained that would tend to promote the comfort and joy of existence; and those who were high in the scale of spiritual attainments could, with this word, perform miracles. This was the belief, and this is still the belief among nearly all who recognize divine power in man. But what this word really is, is a mystery in the minds of the many, and therefore it is usually called the lost word.

The great word is not a word, as many suppose, nor a definite statement of truth. The great word is the soul of every word, the spirit of every thought and the inner power of every expressed statement. In the minds of the great majority it is a lost word, because their speech does not have soul, their thought does not have spirit, and their statements of truth, or untruth, are devoid of inner power. But those who are learning to live, think and act, not as material personalities, but as Sons of God, are finding the great word; they are beginning to speak with authority, and there is hidden power in everything they say. What they say will come true, does come true; what they think they can do they gain the power to do, and their word invariably contains some exceptional quality that the ordinary mind cannot define. The spiritually minded, however, can understand; they know the secret; they realize that the great word is the supreme power of divine being coming forth into the speech, the thought and the actions of the fully awakened soul. And if these minds will continue to enter more and more deeply into the spirit of this supreme power they will find that the great word can do everything that the ages have declared that it could do. Thousands today do, at times, use this secret word; that is, they give soul to what they say, and they give spirit to what they think; in consequence, their words carry weight and their thoughts have extraordinary power. But they do not, as a rule, understand how the power of the soul is given to word and thought, and therefore do not secure results whenever they may so desire. The secret, however, is simple, so simple that it can be comprehended and applied by anyone.

To begin, train yourself to feel inner power whenever you give expression to a statement of truth; and whenever you think enter into the spirit of your thought. When you speak, do not simply say words; say more. Never indulge in empty speech; that is, place yourself, your whole self, your great self into every word you utter. Let the spoken word be the body of your speech, but see that every body has a great soul. The audible word itself has no power, but that word can carry all the power that you can inwardly feel at the time it is spoken. When you give soul to your speech every word will contain hidden power, and it is this hidden power of the spoken word that constitutes the secret word, the great word, the word that works wonders for those who understand. We realize, therefore, that there is nothing mystical or mysterious about the great word; it is simply a measure of supreme spiritual power taking expression in thought or speech. Jesus Christ was the greatest master in the use of the word that we know, though there have been hundreds in every age that have discerned its power and applied it to a great degree. In this age there are more than there ever were before who are consciously using the word, but as the general understanding of its nature is not clear, results are not as great as they might be. But it is predicted that we are to do the greater works, and it is our privilege to do so now because we have received the power.

There are thousands in the world today who are ready to do the greater works; they understand the law; they know the truth and their desire to live the truth is becoming stronger every hour; but there is one thing more needful. We must enter more deeply into the spirit. To believe in things spiritual is not sufficient; nor will the daily effort to conform with spiritual principles supply the necessary requirements. We must do all of these things and more. We must aim to enter into the very life of the innermost power of the spirit whatever we think, say or do. When we think the truth, we must mentally feel the inner spirit of that truth. When we desire the realization of some divine quality or perfect condition, we must mentally feel the deep invincible soul of that desire. And when we speak, we must not speak as personal men, but as spiritual Sons of the Most High, endued with limitless power from the Supreme. In brief, whatever we do in body, mind or soul, we must enter more deeply into the hidden powers of the spirit, and must try to realize that that power is the very soul of all power. When we think we can feel the soul of divine power, we must try to enter into the soul of that soul; and when we realize that a deeper soul state is being felt, we must try to enter into the soul of this deeper state, and so on, ever going deeper and deeper into the limitless vastness of the spirit. Thus we shall gain the great word, the word that gives soul to every word, spirit to every thought and inner power to every statement.

Give soul to every spoken word and you can heal yourself by saying, "I Am Well"; you can emancipate yourself from every adverse condition by saying, "I Am the Freedom of Divine Truth"; and you can cause every atom in your being to thrill with life and power by saying, "I Am the Strength of the Infinite." Give spirit to every thought you think and every condition you picture in the mind will be realized in the body. Every true desire you feel will be fulfilled, and every dream of greater things will positively come true. What you think you can do you will gain the power to do, because every thought that is filled with the spirit is also filled with the limitless power of the spirit. Give inner power to every statement, and whatever you affirm to be true you will cause to come true. The great word is creative, and if the hidden power of this word is in your statement, it will create whatever your statement may affirm. Therefore, select your statements with wisdom, and pray only for that which you know that you want. When you regain the lost word, all your prayers will be answered and all your desires come true. It is therefore advisable to pray for wisdom first, to desire spirituality first, and to seek first the kingdom of God.

The power of the spirit finds full expression only through the Word; but since mankind in general does not possess the Word, it is usually spoken of as the "lost word." To the mind that is only partly awakened this Word is something vague, almost incomprehensible, yet a jewel most earnestly desired. He feels that there is something within him that can know this Word, and speak the Word, but it seems to be lost to his mind in some mysterious manner. It is the speaking of the Word, however, that heals the sick and that makes man free; it is therefore most desirable to possess. When it is stated that the Word is lost, the idea is not that the human race possessed it once, and lost it later. The entire race never did possess the Word, never had the power to speak the Word. The Word has been lost to the race from the beginning of manifested existence in this sphere, but has been found in every age by the illumined minds of that age, and through those minds declared to the world. Instead of speaking of the Word as the "lost word," it would therefore be better to speak of it as the "hidden word," hidden from the mind of personal man, but revealed to the minds of illumined souls.

Those minds that are on the borderland of the great awakening realize that immediately beyond their present mental comprehension lies a world of wisdom and light, indescribable in its marvelousness and beauty. To some minds it is so near that at times the veil is parted, and they obtain a slight glimpse of the glory and splendor that was, is and is to be. Others have crossed the border at certain periods in their lives and have actually entered, for a time, the Father's House of the Many Mansions. But the great purpose of every soul is to some day enter this celestial world and abide there always. Many have believed that we must leave the body before we can enter that sublime realm; the truth is, however, that we may enter today, if we are ready, and live in that higher world while still living upon earth in physical form. We shall then find that the earth is not outside of the kingdom, but that the real earth, spiritually discerned and understood in truth, is also one of His secret places.

To have the spiritual discernment to look into this beautiful world, these higher realms, and behold the sublime glory of the kingdom, the Father's House of the Many Mansions, is to regain the "lost word." "It is for you to know the mysteries of the kingdom"; and whoever has sufficient spiritual power to part the veil and see those things that are prepared for them that love Him, has found the "hidden word." Now he knows the mysteries; he has seen them as they are. He has crossed the border, he has trod the shining shore and his eyes have beheld eternity. He has seen the Word, because the One Divine Word is the revelation of all that Is Eternal. Whoever can see that which Eternally Is, that to which nothing can be added, nothing taken away, that which is the foundation of all, the life of all, the all in all, can see the Word. The Word is revealed to him; divine wisdom has inspired his soul, the light of the spirit has illumined his mind, and he speaks as one having authority. He speaks, not of that which others have told him, not as the scribes; he has seen the mysteries; he bears witness to the truth because he has witnessed and beheld the truth with his own illumined mind. The heavens have opened before him; he has not only had a vision; he has seen the truth that is beyond the vision and that truth is the Word.

To reach this sublime state the secret is faith; not the faith that believes, but the faith that knows, the faith that can see with the vision of the spirit. Every soul that has some discernment of higher things has a portion of faith. This faith increases as the soul ascends, and the soul ascends as the faith becomes larger, higher and more illumined. To feel the touch of the spirit is the beginning of real faith, and the nearer the soul lives to the spirit the larger the faith. In the first stages of faith, the way is opened for the power of the spirit to come forth and prepare the human temple for the greater things that are to follow. After this period, if the mind continues in spiritual growth, illumination begins, and will continue until the Christ state is attained.

During the first stages of spiritual illumination the mind feels the nearness of a higher world, and here is the soul's opportunity to take many steps towards the heights. Whenever these sublime moments appear, enter the stillness of the spirit, and place body, mind and thought in touch with the soul's eternal calm. Then when in the peace that passeth understanding, open the eyes of the spirit, and in faith, desire to meet Him face to face. He may not appear; but be not impatient; know that He will appear, and you can wait. You can wait an eternity for such a privilege, for a single moment in His Presence is a million heavens in one. But when you do draw near enough to behold His shining glory, give thanks with all the power of heart and soul. The Redeemer has entered your life; you have found the way; you have entered the great climax of human existence and now you may begin to live. Henceforth, give your highest thought and attention to every spiritual experience that may appear, no matter how insignificant it may seem to be. Know that every manifestation of Divine Presence indicates that you are growing in the spirit, that your spiritual eyes are being opened, that you are beginning to discern His omnipresence and to know that He is always here, closer than breathing, nearer than hands and feet.

To know God is the beginning of all wisdom. To know and feel that God is here, everywhere, that we live in His spirit, His life, His wisdom, His power, His light and His love now, is to awaken the mind to real wisdom. Then we shall find the "hidden word"; then we shall enter the inner sanctuary of the soul and behold the Word of God manifested in the true being of man, eternally creating the true being of man in the likeness of the image divine. And then we behold the Word of truth in the being of truth we gain the power to speak the Word of truth. To know the lord is to have the power to speak the Word, and to speak the Word is to cause the Word to become flesh. Thus the life, the wholeness and the glory of the spirit is made real in the personal being of man.

To grow daily in the spirit is the way to the higher faith, the larger wisdom and the beautiful life. Aspire constantly to live the life of the spirit; turn all thought and attention to the more perfect understanding of the spirit; keep the eye single upon the divine perfection of the spirit, and there shall be many moments when His spirit will actually appear. When these moments come, grieve not the spirit away; receive its life and its power by entering into the stillness within; then open widely the door of the heart that the Guest from On High may come in. Soon He will come again. His coming will become more and more frequent, and when you are ready to actually live the life He lives, He will not go away any more.

Whenever the spirit comes and is received, the Word is being revealed to you and you obtain a larger glimpse of that sublime state of being where you are about to enter, never to return. Never to return to the ways of the world; never to return to the bondage of sin; but to live in the light and the freedom of the spirit while still in personal form; to walk with God while still walking the earth; to be surrounded and protected by His invisible power while still living and working in the midst of visible things. In the world and yet above the world. Whenever you discern more clearly the glory of the kingdom it means that you are drawing nearer and nearer to the pearly gates. Press on; not with force and will, but with peace and faith, the eye ever single upon the Light that leads. It is the will of God that we should enter now "another and a better world." That world is not a future state of existence, but an eternal state of existence; it is therefore at hand here and now. To enter the "pearly gates" is to enter that better world, God's own true world where all is well. And those gates are ajar to all who can speak the Word.

Light within, guide thou my way,
I am seeking truth today;
Where thou leadest I will go,
And all wisdom I shall know.
Peace and joy and truth and love
Are the blessings from above
That will surely come to me
When I gently follow thee.

Light within, thou light divine,
Thou shalt never cease to shine;
Thou canst not depart from me;
We are one, for I am thee.
Darkness flies and sins depart,
Truth is reigning in my heart;
Endless day dispersed the night
When I found I was the Light.

CHAPTER XIII

The Royal Path to Wisdom

Solomon prayed for wisdom and received it; any other soul may do the same. God is infinite wisdom; and "all that the Father hath is mine"; we need simply go and receive our own. We may receive from the supreme mind, at any time, as much wisdom on any subject as our own minds can possibly appropriate, and we may also receive, from the same source, the power to appropriate more.

The wisdom that comes from God does not simply pertain to the soul or to the life of some other world, because God is the original source of all wisdom, and therefore we may receive light directly from Him on any subject whatever. Nor does the wisdom that comes from God need special interpretation; it is sufficiently clear for anyone to understand who is in harmony with God.

When higher wisdom needs interpretation, it is not from God, but is simply the mystical ideas of minds that have not found the clear light of the Infinite mind. The mystical wisdom of man is complex and confusing; the wisdom of God is simple and illuminating; the former produces darkness and doubt; the latter produces that faith that knows.

When we learn that real wisdom comes directly from God, we shall no longer seek knowledge through the training of the senses to discriminate between illusions; nor shall we depend upon experience for instruction. Real wisdom does not come from experience; experience can only tell us how it feels to live in illusions and overcome illusions, but it tells us nothing about how it feels to live in the real and ascend into the greater and greater life of the real.

The mind that lives in the light of the Most High knows the result of any experience long before that experience arrives; therefore, to such a mind, experience can convey no information. If the experience is pleasant, it is welcomed and received for the joy it brings, but if it is not pleasant, it is avoided, and the mind that is taught of God knows beforehand whether any particular experience will be desirable or not.

To live with God is to gain good from every source, be the source physical, mental or spiritual; but the wisdom that comes with this good does not come from these various sources; it may come through these sources because to live with God is to touch God everywhere, and thus receive wisdom from God through every channel in the world.

To be taught of God is to pray for wisdom, to depend upon God for wisdom, and to live so near to God that we shall be in the light of His wisdom. Whatever we wish to know, we should take it to God, and let His spirit lead us, guide us, and inspire our minds with the truth desired.

The mind that is led by the spirit will not go wrong; or if it should temporarily be on the verge of taking a misstep, something will interfere. This something may seem to be special providence, and in a certain sense it is, because the Infinite is ever ready to do for man whatever he may wish to have done.

When we place ourselves in the hands of the Infinite, He will find a way, and this way will be revealed to us before it is too late. Sometimes it may not appear until the eleventh hour, but it invariably comes in time. We may therefore rest assured in this faith and know "that I will not forsake thee nor leave thee; I am thy Redeemer, I will care for thee."

The great secret of all the inspired minds of the ages may be found here; they seemed to have superhuman knowledge, they spoke with authority, and their words have been universally received as the truth; the reason being, they lived in the light of the Most High; they were taught of God.

To be taught of God it is necessary to live with God, walk with God, and open the mind completely to the great influx of supreme light from on high. It is necessary to be in such close spiritual touch with the Infinite mind that we can feel the thought of God and think His thoughts after Him. And this any soul can do. To live with God is the simplest life of all and also the most beautiful; and to walk with God requires no effort whatever. Any soul that can lift up the mind toward supreme spiritual realms can walk with God now.

When we place ourselves in that position where we can be taught of God, it is then that we begin to use the mind in the highest sense. It is then that the mind becomes so transparent that the light of Infinite wisdom can shine through and manifest itself in all its brilliancy and glory. It is then that the Word becomes flesh, and the truth of divine being is unfolded in the personal life of man.

The true function of the human mind is to think with the Infinite mind, because the human mind is an inseparable part of the Infinite mind. When the human mind tries to think alone, it becomes confused, and the ideas that it may form are mere illusions.

It is therefore evident that all the ideas in the world that have been formed while the human mind was trying to think apart from the Infinite mind are illusions; and the wisdom of the world is full of such illusions. We can remove them completely, however, by turning to God and opening our minds completely to the clear light from on high.

When we begin to receive the wisdom of God, we find that the wisdom of the world was the cause of our trouble; we were living in darkness and could not see the way, therefore took many missteps and made many mistakes; but when we open our minds to the wisdom of God we are in the light, the way is clear, and we shall not go wrong any more.

However, we are not required to ignore everything that man may say in order to receive the pure wisdom of God. God speaks through everything and most of all through man. When we desire, with the whole heart, to be taught of God, we shall constantly receive wisdom from God, and it may come through a million channels, including the mind of man, but we must remember that the mind of man does not simply mean the minds of other men; our own minds are included in the mind of man, and as we grow in the spirit we shall receive most of our divine wisdom with our own mentalities as the principal channel.

This is the great goal we have in view, but we cannot place our own minds in perfect touch with the Infinite mind unless we think of all minds and all things as being channels for the wisdom of God. When we can see God in all things, then we shall meet Him face to face. When we can receive His wisdom through all things, then we shall hear His voice speaking directly to us in the beautiful silence of our own soul.

When we enter this silence, as we may at any time, we know we are in communication with God, and we may learn the truth about anything that we have sought to understand. God is not a God of the future state alone. He is the God of all time, even the present, and He is at hand ready to lead us aright in everything that we may wish to do in the present. We may be taught now by Him in all things pertaining to physical and mental existence as well as the very highest spiritual existence. And the more we ask of God the more we please God.

"Lay not up for yourself treasures upon earth." Where the heart is there our treasures will be also, and when the heart is in the earth, earthy, all that is beautiful in life will be lost. Our treasure is that which we love the best, but it is not wisdom to give our best love to things. Give your best love to the spirit of things and you will receive, not only the visible form, but also that sublime something that gives life and loveliness to the form. Seek the riches of the spirit and you gain wealth and happiness that shall never pass away. The richest man in the world is he who has found the diamond fields of the soul, while the poorest is he who is burdened with things that have not the spirit of things. It is our privilege to have abundance of all that is rich and beautiful in the visible world, but it is the wealth and the beauty of the soul that gives happiness; it is the treasures we lay up in the spiritual within that make all other treasures worthwhile.

When we know that God is life, power, health, harmony and joy, we will receive those blessings in boundless supply whenever we feel that His presence is here. When we attain the consciousness of the omnipresence of God, we will receive from God whatever we know to be in God.

CHAPTER XIV

The Golden Path to Increase

For whosoever hath, to him shall be given, and
he shall have abundance; but whosoever
hath not, from him shall be taken
away even that which he hath.
—MAT. 13:12.

The real element of possession exists in consciousness. What we possess in consciousness we inevitably will gain in the personal life; and no matter how well secured our external possessions may be, the moment we begin to feel in conscious that we may lose them, our hold on those things will weaken, and external loss will shortly begin unless this adverse state of mind is immediately changed.

To consciously feel that everything you need or desire is for you—in brief, actually belongs to you in the real is to be among those that hath, even though you may at present be empty handed in the external world. To you shall be given, and you shall have abundance both in spiritual possessions and in visible possessions.

But to consciously feel that you do not have real or permanent possession of anything is to be among those that hath not, even though you may have visible wealth in great measure. From you shall be taken away, and those external possessions that you seem to have shall pass to other hands.

This law is universal in its application and holds true in all matters, be they physical, mental or spiritual. The secret of gaining more on any plane is to consciously feel that you have more. Enter into the "hath" state of mind. Whether you desire life, health, power, wisdom, spirituality or greater abundance in external things, train your consciousness to feel that you have the real substance of the thing desired. Do not judge according to appearances, but continue to inwardly feel the possession of that which you claim as your possession.

When the mind enters the feeling of conscious possession, the first gain is the fuller possession of yourself and your powers; you immediately begin to feel stronger; this will strengthen and enlarge your consciousness of gain, which in turn will increase the power of accumulation that has begun in your system. You thus not only become larger and stronger in your own nature, but you gain a more powerful hold upon everything with which you may come in contact. You awaken greater and superior qualities in your own mind and soul, and you inspire faith and confidence in the minds of others. You thus create those advantages and essentials, both in the within and in the without, that are conducive to gain.

When the mind enters the fear of loss and begins to feel that there is going to be loss, the first loss is the loss of self-possession. You lose your hold upon your own powers and, in consequence, begin to weaken. Your faculties fail to do their best, your work becomes inferior, your personality does not attract as it did, and your power to inspire confidence in others is on the wane. You suffer loss in all things, physical, mental and spiritual, and you are daily losing ground. Finally, everything that you seemed to possess is taken away. But the loss began in your own consciousness, and you could have stopped it there if you had known how.

The losing tendency can be stopped at any stage, but the only place where it can be immediately stopped is at its first appearance in consciousness. When you begin to feel that there is danger of loss, or when the general indications seem to predict loss, remove that feeling at once. Refuse to think of loss; refuse to admit the possibility of loss; refuse to recognize loss in any form whatever. Proceed to claim your own; give all the power of mind and thought to the great truth that you do possess now, in the real, everything that you can possibly need or desire. Give full recognition to the boundlessness of your own spiritual riches, and live in the conviction that whatever you claim possession of in the within you will gain possession of in the without.

The tide will turn before any real loss takes place; and instead of falling back into the world of the ones that hath not, you will advance farther into the richness of that world where dwell the ones that hath. In consequence, to you will be given, and you will have more than you ever had before. This method should be used with faith and perseverance whenever there is the least indication of loss; negative conditions should be replaced with positive conditions, fear should be annihilated by faith, and every downward tendency should be converted into a strong ascending tendency.

To live in the "hath" state of mind and grow steadily in the conscious feeling of possession, continuous growth in spirituality will be required. It is only through spirituality that we can grasp the reality of the inner substance of things, and we must gain consciousness of the inner substance of life before we can master those forces that make for perpetual increase in life.

To live in the "hath" state of mind it is also necessary to advance constantly into a deeper and larger conscious possession of those things that we already possess in abundance. There can be no inaction in consciousness; if we are not going forward into the larger and the more perfect we are going back and down into the lesser. Therefore, no matter how much power we actually possess, we should daily claim conscious possession of more; no matter how perfect our health may be, we should daily enter into the consciousness of higher perfections of health. When we cease to grow in health we prepare the system for sickness, but so long as we grow in health, sickness will be impossible.

The same law is applicable both to external possessions and spiritual possessions. To retain what we have we must daily develop the consciousness of more. The moment we decide to be satisfied with what we have we will begin to lose what we have. There is no limit to the riches of the kingdom of life, and it is the will of God that man shall enjoy more and more of these riches, every day, so long as eternity shall continue to be. And to do the will of God is to bring the highest happiness to man.

That the love of money is the root of all evil is true, providing we give the statement its true and full significance. When we speak of money we do not mean those things simply that pass for money, but we mean all external possessions. When we love external possessions the heart is in the without and not in the spirit as it always should be to be in the truth. When the heart is in external things, we begin to live for things; the mind comes to the surface and consequently becomes shallow and material. The mind that lives on the surface is not in touch with the deep things of life, is not conscious of the inner light of truth, and is therefore in darkness. To be in darkness is to go wrong, and to go wrong is to create evil. Every mind that is not led by the inner light of the spirit will go wrong; in fact, every wrong act comes because the mind follows external darkness instead of internal light; and it is only the love of other things that draws the mind out into the darkness of things. So long as we love the spirit the mind is in touch with the spirit and is illumined by the light of the spirit. When we are in this light we will not go wrong; we will not commit evil, because we can see the right, and we can see that the right is the very thing we have desired, longed for, prayed for.

The more deeply we love the inner life and the riches of the spirit, the more spiritual and illumined we become; accordingly, we can see more and more clearly how to do all things as they should be done; our mistakes will decrease, and wrongs and evil will disappear. To love the life is to enter into the spirit of truth, and in the truth there is freedom—freedom from sickness, evil, weakness and want. Evil can grow only in materiality; and materiality is produced simply by our own confused thinking. But when we are in touch with the spiritual life within, our thinking is not confused; we are then in the light of truth, and we think the truth. In consequence, we no longer produce the darkness and discord of materiality; instead we produce the peace and the harmony of spirituality, and all is well.

When your treasure, that is, that which you love the best, is in the without, in the earth, earthy, your whole life will be in the earth, earthy. You will thus live continually in wrong thought because you do not see how to create right thought. All mental light, even the light of reason, comes from within; therefore, when the mind is so absorbed in outer things that it ignores completely the within, all thinking will be more or less at variance with truth, and evils must necessarily follow. But when your treasure is in the spirit, and you love the riches of the soul better than anything else, you will live on the mountaintop. You will dwell in realms sublime, in the very light of His infinite wisdom; all your thinking will be illumined with that light; you will thus think only the truth, and he produces no evil who always thinks the truth.

To lay up treasures in heaven is not to prepare for a heaven in the future, but to accumulate greater and greater spiritual riches now. That soul that is attaining real spiritual wisdom, that is growing daily in the love that loves everything, that is living in the peace that passeth understanding, that is being filled more and more with life and power from on high, that is gaining conscious realization of all the divine elements of pure, spiritual being—that soul is laying up treasures in heaven. Such a soul is actually coming into possession of those superior riches now and is learning to use them today for the glory of God and the emancipation of man.

To become a strong soul, to attain the mastery of the spirit, to become a living inspiration to all the world, to unfold all that is lofty and beautiful and sublime in the spiritual life, to realize the joy everlasting and draw nearer and nearer to the Christ state—that is the purpose of him who is laying up treasures in heaven. And when we possess spirituality with all its qualities of high worth, we have the riches of all riches; we have that something that can produce all riches, not only in the spirit, but also in mind and body. That person who has found the riches of the within need never have any fear of external loss. Though all might disappear in the without, still, being in touch with the source of all supply, he could at once begin to regain everything. When we are in the spirit we are upon the solid rock of all good; we possess the key to unbounded riches on all planes, and so long as we live in the spirit we shall not lose that key. When one door closes we can open another, sometimes several, and all that the heart can wish for shall always be ours to possess and enjoy. When we are in the spirit, we not only possess the riches of the spirit—those riches that actually make every moment of existence a full realization of the highest joys of life—but we also possess the power to supply the without abundantly, being in perfect touch with the Giver of all that is good in the world.

There is no truth in the belief that we must necessarily relinquish external possessions the moment we begin to lay up treasures in heaven. That power that produces the riches of the spirit, can and will produce abundance in the external world as well. All outer things will invariably be added when the kingdom within is sought, actually sought, and sought first, not only at first but always. So long as we seek only the treasures of earth we get but little of those treasures, while we get an overabundance of the suffering and pain of material existence. But when we begin to lay up treasures in heaven, we obtain the peace, the joy, the contentment, the health, the strength, the wisdom, the power and the life we so greatly desire; in addition, we obtain higher spiritual possessions without number and an abundance of everything that is necessary to make the outer life full and complete.

Live eternally in conscious unity with the Infinite; have faith in God, have faith in humanity, have faith in yourself; then live, think and act according to principles only, and there is nothing you may not accomplish.

Great deeds in life are invariably brought about by higher power. And if we would be constantly in touch with higher power, we must live in the perfect faith and consciousness of the great spiritual within, where higher power has its center and throne. This, however, is not possible so long as we think more of the person than of the soul. To be centered in the spirit we must live in the spirit, and give the spirit our first thought at all times. Then we shall be filled with the supreme power of the spirit, and our strength, both in mind and body, shall be daily renewed from on high.

"Resist not him that is evil." The true path to emancipation is to give so much thought, life and attention to the building of the good that we have not the time to even think of evil. Then evil will die for want of nourishment. The mind that is absolutely full of a strong, spiritual building power has no room whatever for evil conditions of any kind.

CHAPTER XV

The Life More Abundant

I came that they may have life, and
may have it abundantly:
—John 10:10.

The greatest thing that man can do is to live. Everything that appears in any sphere of existence comes from life, and therefore everything increases with the increase of life. To live more is to become more and gain the power to accomplish more whatever the field of action may be; to live more is to enter more fully into the richness and joy of life itself, and there is no joy that is greater than that which comes from perpetual growth in real life.

The purpose of life is to live more life; the principal secret of perfection in any period of life is to live as large a life as that period can appreciate and employ, and to constantly add to the abundance of that large life is to make each period better than the one that went before. Growth in life means growth in health, growth in strength, growth in capacity, growth in mental brilliancy, growth in talent, growth in wisdom, growth in power, and, in brief, growth in everything that a normal state of existence can possibly need or desire. The mission of the Christ is therefore not purely transcendental, nor solely for some other world.

The teachings of the Christ are applicable to every part of personal existence and may be applied with great profit in every circumstance or event that can arise in the great eternal now. What is more, no person can do full justice to anything he may undertake to do unless he enters into full harmony with the great mission of the Christ. The life more abundant can come only through the Christ, and we all need the life more abundant if we are to be true to our own marvelous nature.

The coming of the Christ, however, was not confined to a short period of time some two thousand years ago; the Christ comes now to every one who enters the spirit; and when He comes, He invariably brings the life more abundant. We may, at any time, enter the fullness of eternal life; and when we do, everything changes for the better. The life more abundant dispels the ills of existence in the same manner as light dispels darkness, and just as effectively, whatever those ills may be.

The ills of personal existence come principally from two causes: ignorance of divine law and false desire. The coming of the life more abundant gives the mind the necessary power to understand the laws of life; when we are in the life eternal we are in harmony with the laws of the life eternal, and will not misuse those laws any more. When we are filled with the richer life from within we no longer desire the lesser things in the without; we will not care for the wrong, having found everything that heart can wish for in the beautiful kingdom of the right.

To enter the life more abundant, first live the teachings of the Christ; not according to the letter but according to the spirit. The spirit is infinitely greater than the letter and includes everything of worth that the letter may contain. Second, live now in the Christ consciousness. Know that the Christ is here, that His spirit is within you and all about you, and that you can be conscious of His presence at any time by simply opening your own mind to His kindness and tenderness and sublime love. Know that "I am with you, even to the end of the world," and think on these things.

The more attention we give to the great truth that the Christ is here with us now, the more we open the mind to the consciousness of His spiritual presence, and as we enter more and more into the consciousness of the Christ, we enter more and more into the limitless life of the Christ; thus we become filled, through and through, with the supreme power of that life that is eternal life.

The life eternal, however, is not distinct from any other form of life; it is the source of all life, and as we enter more and more into the life eternal we gain more life on every plane of being. We then begin to express the life more abundant through every part of body, mind and soul, and thus demonstrate conclusively that a strong soul does not mean a weak body.

The life of the soul is eternal life, and the more we unfold that life the more health, strength and vigor we give to the body; the mind becomes more brilliant, the personality more powerful, and the character more beautiful. And above all, we ascend to that sublime life on the heights that is fairer than ten thousand to the soul.

For whosoever would save his life shall lose it;
and whosoever shall lose his life
for my sake shall find it.
—MAT. 16:25.

When you lose your life for the sake of Christ, you let go of the limited life that is living in you in order that the limitless life of the Christ may live in you. Likewise, when you deny yourself and follow the Christ you remove the personal self from the throne of your being and enthrone the superior spiritual self instead. There is therefore no sacrifice; you lose nothing but your limitations and your illusions, while you gain everything that the kingdom of God holds in store for man.

The belief that it is necessary to lose something of actual value in order to gain the life eternal is not the truth. Poverty in the personal life does not produce spiritual riches, nor does the sacrifice of temporal joys produce the bliss of heaven. The idea of self-sacrifice must be eliminated; so long as we think that we have to sacrifice all that is good in the visible world in order to gain the joys and the riches of the invisible, we are out of harmony with the beautiful order of the cosmos. In the true order of things all that is real is good, and all that is good, man has the privilege to enjoy now.

The only things that we are required to sacrifice are our ills, our defects, our weaknesses, our shortcomings, our limitations; in brief, we are required to remove the personal self and its imperfections from our world of existence. The true self-sacrifice is that which refuses to permit personal imperfections to rule in the personal life, and gives up to the light, the power and the life of the spirit.

When you deny yourself in the true manner, you deny your outer mind the privilege of rulership. You no longer follow the desires and the beliefs of the flesh; you no longer obey the dictates of the body; you declare that the body must serve the soul and the soul must serve the Christ. You thereby permit the supreme life of the Christ to live in you; the mind that was in

Christ Jesus enters your mind, and His life and His power becomes your own. The lesser life is lost, the greater life has come in its place. The mere man in you is decreasing while the divine in you is increasing and will thus continue until you are perfect as your heavenly Father is perfect.

To try to save the personal life is to live exclusively for the limitations of external existence; in consequence, the mind becomes so absorbed in the lesser life without that it is wholly unconscious of the greater life within. But we cannot receive the greater life from within unless we are in conscious touch with that life, and since the within is the only source of life, we cease to receive life the moment we are consciously separated from the inner life.

To live entirely for the personal life is to be separated from the inner life, and therefore we are not receiving any more life. The personal life, however, that we are trying to save will be gradually used up, and thus we will lose what we are so anxious to save. But when we begin to live for the spirit and begin to follow the Christ into the vast spiritual realms of limitless life, we will find more and more life; and the more life we find in the vast within the more life we will bring forth into the without. All the life that we become conscious of in the soul we will express in the mind and the body, and the personal self, instead of growing weaker, will grow stronger and stronger as it is filled more and more with life and power from on high. And thus, by losing ourselves in Christ we gain everything that exists in the supreme life of the Christ; we lose nothing, sacrifice nothing, while we find ourselves—all that we are in the image and likeness of God.

Live a beautiful life wherever you may be and you become a living benediction to all who may pass your way. You may see no immediate results; in fact, your beautiful life may have scattered its blessings so far and wide that you cannot find the exact places where the flowers grow that you planted; but that does not matter. You have given; in consequence, the world is better off and you are a stronger soul. You know that not a single good deed can be lost; somewhere it will bless somebody. You know that every good seed that you may sow in the garden of human life will someday take root and grow. You may not remain long enough to see the flowers, but somebody will see those flowers, and the fact that your hand planted the seed is pleasure enough for you. To feel that you have given happiness to someone else is the greatest happiness of all; and to know that millions will be inspired by the sublimity of your life ages after you are gone—could anything give a deeper joy to the soul? And yet, this is a privilege that is not given only to the few; there is not a soul that may not look forward to such a future and to such a life.

To be perfectly satisfied to let your light shine wherever you may go without ever looking back to see if there were results or no, is the mark of a great soul. So long as we do not wish to give unless we see visible results in exact places, our spirituality is not of the greatest; and so long as we require the personal testimony of those whom we have helped, to spur us on, our faith is nothing. He who has the true faith knows that spiritual living is a power wherever it is lived, and he never thinks of looking back to find if it was true. He scatters the seed and leaves results to Him that faileth not. He radiates the good and knows that that which is good can never cease to produce good.

When you realize that you are an entity through which God is expressed and that your mind should be so transparent that the highest divine light may shine through and illumine the outer world, you have found your true place. To remain constantly in that beautiful place means that a higher power will be flowing through your being, radiating in every direction, giving the spirit of truth to everything you may think, say or do. You thus become a personal expression of the Word, and your life will be a message of truth to the race.

"Ye are the light of the world." Do not hide your spirituality in your feelings or your emotions. There is power in the spirit. Live this power and give personal expression to everything that the spirit may contain. Then you will demonstrate to the world that the way of the spirit is the true way. When you are lifted up, hundreds and even thousands will come and go where you are going. Therefore, let the full glory of the spirit shine in your life; let power from on high manifest itself in everything that you may think or say or do, and great shall be your reward, both in this world and in the world to come. The spiritual life deprives you of nothing that has real worth and gives you more and more of everything that has high worth.

"Agree with thine adversary quickly." There is a spiritual side to everything; enter into harmony with this spiritual side and the discord that seems to exist on the personal side will disappear. Forget those elements that are at variance and think only of those states that are perfectly at one with each other. You can easily find them; we find everything we seek, and whoever goes out to find harmony will discover that there is more harmony in the world than anything else, excepting life itself.

CHAPTER XVI

Human Nature Becoming Divine Nature

There are thousands of people in the world today who have undertaken to live the spiritual life, and the majority of them understand, to a fair degree, the principles upon which such a life is based; nevertheless, there are too many who do not have as great results as they ought to have, and they are at a loss to find the reason why. With the spiritual wisdom which we now possess, we ought to do greater things than were ever known upon earth before; we ought to be able to overcome every wrong, not only in our own lives, but also in the lives of all who are receptive to our spiritual work; and we ought to realize an ever-increasing abundance of infinite good and infinite power from on high. We ought to do all these things and much more, and when we can see distinctly where the two ways part, we certainly shall.

When we know that we have such an exceptional opportunity for higher usefulness in this age, we cannot be satisfied simply to use the power of divine truth for the attainment of physical health and personal prosperity. There are other and greater things to work for, but not many have the secret path to the world of these greater things. However, the reason why is simple; and likewise, the reason why the majority do not secure as great results as they should in the lesser things is also simple. And the reason is we cannot serve two masters; we cannot take two paths at the same time; when we come to the parting of the ways we must take the one that leads into light and forget the other absolutely.

When we learn that man is created in the image and likeness of God, we enter a new realm of thought; we have made a new discovery, and we have found another way to think and live. The former belief taught us to think and live as a sinner, as a weak human body; the new truth has taught us to live as a spiritual being, as a child of God, as a strong, perfect, divine soul. And here is the place where we must decide which way to go, as it is not possible to believe the old and the new at the same time and have result; nor is it possible to believe part of the old and part of the new at the same time and realize that power for good that the new may contain.

There are many minds who believe in divine truth, and who accept fully the great truth that man is the image of God, but still continue to think of themselves as weak human creatures. When the difficult task comes, and they fail, they usually become discouraged, and this is their language: "Just as I expected; but then I am only human, only a weak, frail, being, not able to cope with these things; some day I may be able to overcome, but as yet I am too weak; I must not expect too much of myself, as I am only human." This is the drift of the thought in many a mind, and it explains perfectly why they have not overcome the wrong and attained the good. They are trying to realize the perfection of the divine within while recognizing the imperfection of the human without. They expect to attain divine power while persisting in living in the world of human weakness. They are trying to serve both the truth and the untruth, but we cannot realize the power of truth until we eliminate the untruth completely.

The outer has seemed to be the only reality so long that the mind naturally thinks everything existing in the outer to be reality; and here is the difficulty. We think the outer to be substantial and the inner to be "mere mental mist," but it is when we reverse this belief that we find the real truth. The statement that the flesh is weak has been a race thought for ages, and it comes natural to think of the flesh as weak; but the truth is that the flesh is weak because we have made it so, and we have made is so by claiming human weakness as our heritage instead of spiritual strength. He who lives constantly in the conviction that unbounded, spiritual strength is his inheritance now will never for one moment feel that the flesh is weak. The flesh is what we make it, and it is just as easy to make it strong as to make it weak. Think that you are a weak, frail human creature and the flesh will become the dwelling place of weakness; but know that you are a strong, invincible, eternal soul, and the flesh will become the very embodiment of strength and will be filled with life and power from on high.

We may philosophize learnedly about the beauty of spiritual thought, but that will serve no purpose unless the truth that is contained in our spiritual thought is stamped upon every word we express. We all realize the power of words; whenever we speak we send a life current through every part of the body;

and if the words spoken are the expressions of material belief we give conditions of weakness to the body, and at times even disease. When we stamp every word, not with human thought, but with divine thought, every word will convey to the person the very spirit of life, power and wholeness. Through the power of speech a person can bring upon himself every wrong in the world; and through the same power he can bring upon himself every good in the world. Through the right use of words, uttered or unexpressed, a person can attain or obtain anything. Words are living forces; they create according to their nature, and they attract their kind. When we become as scrupulous about our words as we are about our clothes we shall become a superior race.

The parting of the ways is found where we can see the difference between human expression and divine expression. So long as our expressions are stamped with the belief that we are weak, frail or "only human," we shall continue in weakness and in that smallness of character that we call human nature. But human nature is simply an undeveloped condition; it is not a permanent factor in human existence; it seems to be permanent simply because practically no effort has been given to the unfoldment and expression of man's divine nature. To say that we are "human" and that we must ever remain so in this world is not only the untruth, but such expressions give weakness and adverse conditions to the personal life. We cause the flesh to become weak and remain weak by living in the belief that we are mere human creatures, and therefore when we meet adversity we "fall down," become sick, or otherwise manifest the imperfection of that life that is lived apart from the spirit.

When we take the other path, however, and begin to recognize our divine nature as our only nature, there will soon be a change in events. When this path is taken we recognize limitations no more, and the term "cannot" is forgotten. You never again permit yourself to say that you are sick, tired, limited, easily tempted or merely human. Such expressions you simply will not employ under any circumstances whatever. You know your divine nature, and every thought you think and every word you speak must express what you know to be true. Your every expression of mind, tongue or being thrills with the life and the power of eternal spirit. Regardless of obstacles or adverse events, you stand by your convictions of truth whatever may happen or no. It matters not to you what happens in the exterior. You are not an exterior being; you are a spiritual being, created in the image of God. Nothing that happens can affect you, disturb you, or even touch you; you are in Him, in everlasting safety. You live in the spirit; you know what is true in the spirit, and you think and speak accordingly every moment of your endless existence. Ere long the word of truth becomes a living power in body, mind and soul, and your entire being becomes a perfect expression of that Divine Word that is of God.

There is a strong tendency to compromise with the undeveloped side of the person whenever we fail to demonstrate the absolute power of the spirit. But this must never be permitted. No matter how many times you fail in the person do not admit that you are weak. You are not the person; you are the soul, the perfect image of God, and the image of God is supreme strength regardless of what may happen in the person. Continue to think the absolute truth, even in the midst of sickness, failure, trouble and want, and those things will soon depart never to return any more.

Father I am one with thee,
One through all eternity;
One forever in the past,
One as long as time shall last.
Thou in me and I in thee,
Life of endless unity;
This my dearest song shall be,
Father, I am one with thee.

Father, I am one with thee,
Sweetest thought of truth to me.
I am filled with life divine,
Therefore boundless good is mine.
All my life is lived in thee,
Perfect life of harmony;
This my highest thought shall be,
Father, I am one with thee.

CHAPTER XVII

A Sublime
State of Existence

There never existed an awakened soul that did not believe in a spiritual state of being; and there never existed a soul in any condition of human understanding that did not have glimpses at times of what appeared to be another world. To those who had simply gained the simplest form of human consciousness, this other world seemed to be far away, a place we could not inherit until we had taken our departure from this visible state of existence; but to those who were on the verge of spiritual consciousness, this other world was not a far away place. Those awakened souls could discern that it was a spiritual realm in which all might dwell today—the kingdom of heaven that is ever at hand.

This other world is the soul of the universe, permeating the limitless vastness of the entire cosmos. It is the sublime essence of all reality, the real reality of all that is; it is the infinite spiritual sea in which we live and move and have our being, the divine counterpart of everything that was, is, or is to be. It is that world which we find on the supreme heights of all existence, and is therefore the cosmic world, orderly, harmonious, complete, perfect, transcendent, infinite, divine. To live in this cosmic world is to view the entire universe from the heights, and from that sublime view everything is beautiful and all is good. Therefore, the life of the cosmic is a life of perfected being, everlasting peace and eternal joy. It is the life victorious—the life of the spirit—that every exalted soul has revealed to man, but it is not a life that is apart from personal existence; it is the soul of personal existence.

The cosmic world permeates the physical world as spirit permeates substance; and what the physical world is to the body, the cosmic world is to the soul. According to the true purpose of life, the body should live in the physical world, enjoying everything that is good and beautiful in personal existence; while the soul should live in the cosmic world, enjoying everything that is good and beautiful in spiritual existence. This is complete existence, but the soul cannot consciously live in the cosmic until it is awakened, or until it has become conscious of its own exalted divinity.

The awakening of the soul into the world of its own spiritual nature will not deprive the body of anything that is worthy in physical life. We are not required to leave the physical to enjoy the spiritual, nor is it necessary to sacrifice anything that can add to the welfare of the body in order to inherit the riches of the soul. The greatest good comes into the whole of life only when the body lives a complete physical life and the soul a complete spiritual life. The soul cannot fully express itself unless physical existence is all that it can be on the physical plane, and the body is not fully alive until the soul is awakened on the spiritual plane. We do not appreciate the beauty of the physical until we are illumined by the light of the spiritual, and we cannot comprehend the marvelousness of the visible world until we can see its splendor and vastness from the supreme heights of the cosmic world.

We must live in the cosmic world before we can live real life in any world. It is the soul of existence that unfolds the real beauty, the real worth and the real joy of every form of existence, but we do not become conscious of the soul of existence until we begin to live in the cosmic world. We cannot realize the fullness of life until we live in the source of life, and the source of life is spiritual. All life comes from above, therefore the nearer we live to that which is above, the more life we shall receive until we inherit real life itself—the life of the spirit—the life that is lived in the full consciousness of divine being. When we live almost wholly in the personal we live only in part, but when we live in the full consciousness of the spiritual as well as the personal, that which is in part passes away and the limitless life is realized instead. It is then that we inherit the life more abundant, and everything that life has the power to give.

To live in the cosmic world is to realize the purity and the absoluteness of the spiritual, the divinity of man's real nature and the absolute perfection of his true being. It is to know the truth about man—the truth that he is created in the image and likeness of God, and it is the knowing of this truth that makes man free, that produces complete emancipation. To enter into the cosmic world, therefore, is to enter into freedom, health, harmony and wholeness, and in brief everything that promotes the highest good for body, mind and soul. The cosmic life is the apex of all ascending life, the fulfillment of every true desire in life, the realization of everything that is ideal in life, the attainment of the one supreme goal in the living of divine life. To live in the cosmic is to live in the world of the great within, in the highest state of being, in the life of the soul, in tune with the Infinite, in the secret places of the Most High.

To enter the cosmic world is to ascend to the heights and live the spiritual life. The living of the spiritual life means the overcoming of spiritual death, and it is spiritual death that must be overcome before man can receive his inheritance, here or hereafter. The phenomena of physical death need not concern us; its coming produces no permanent effect upon real existence, nor is anything gained by prolonging personal existence so long as the soul is dead to spiritual existence. It is spiritual life that gives real worth to personal life, and it is the life of the living soul that prolongs indefinitely the life of the living body.

When the soul is not awakened, consciousness lives in a condition of spiritual death and mental darkness. The mind is deprived of the guidance of the spirit and therefore follows blindly the changing desires of the flesh, those desires that are suggested by the world of things. In consequence, the person is almost buried in materiality and goes wrong more frequently than otherwise, usually not knowing the reason why. The result is sickness, trouble and adversity, or the sum total of the ills of life. The real cause of all these ills is spiritual death and the great, infallible remedy is the spiritual life. The ills of life are produced by the mind going wrong, but the mind will not go wrong when it is led by the spirit, and the mind invariably is led by the spirit when we live in the life of the spirit.

The higher we ascend in the true light of the spiritual life the more clearly we can see how to so live that we may be in perfect harmony with all the principles and laws of life. Our sins will cease, our mistakes will diminish, and consequently ill effects will become more and more insignificant until we can truthfully say that we have gained complete emancipation. When we live in the spirit we live in the light, and when we live in the light we will not go wrong. We can then see where to find the greatest good, and no person will seek the lesser after having learned where to find the greater.

When consciousness acts almost entirely in conditions of spiritual death, nearly every action is at variance with the true order of things; in consequence, confusion, darkness and the downfall of the person follows. We always go down when darkness becomes our only guide, and as the spiritual light is the only guiding light, we will continue to go down so long as the spirit is not awakened. When spiritual death begins, downfall begins, not only in the lives of individuals, but also in the lives of nations, races and systems of thought. Therefore, the overcoming of spiritual death is the great hope of the world. It is this alone that can lead us out of the Egypt of sin, sickness, adversity and pain, into the promised land of peace, wholeness, happiness, freedom, power and truth. It is the awakening of the spirit that will take men and nations out of the powers of darkness and place the whole of mankind upon those sublime heights where we shall live a life that is befitting the Sons of God.

The spiritualization of the world means the real salvation of the world; not salvation for the future alone but also salvation from sin, sickness and adversity now. When spiritualization begins, the mind is given a light, and that light invariably leads upward and onward into better things. To spiritualize the mind, the soul must be awakened, and to awaken the soul is to overcome and eliminate the conditions of spiritual death. Then real life begins—the life of an emancipated personal existence harmoniously blended with the life of an exalted spiritual existence.

To awaken the soul, every act of consciousness must be animated with a strong, deeply felt desire to reach the heights; the eye must be kept single upon the supreme spiritual goal, and every thought must be formed by the highest spiritual understanding that can possibly be realized. To live must be the one ruling purpose, and that purpose must be inspired by the spiritual touch of that life that we know to be eternal life.

To awaken the soul and illumine the mind with the light of the spirit, one of the great essentials is to live by faith. To live by faith is to place your entire life and everything that pertains to your life in the hands of Supreme Power. This means that your life will be drawn towards the heights, because Supreme Power is ever ascending toward greater and greater heights. It also means that all things that pertain to your life will work together for the greatest good, because it is the purpose of Supreme Power to produce the greatest good. Whatever is placed in the hands of this power will be inspired and guided by this power, and consequently will do what this power is doing, that is, working in harmony with everything to produce the greatest good.

The secret of faith is therefore simple, and we can readily understand why all things become possible to him who has real faith. Supreme Power can do all things, and he who has faith places his life, his purpose, his plans, his desires - everything—in the hands of Supreme Power. That he should fail is impossible. When the Supreme is with us nothing can be against us, and the Supreme is with us when we place ourselves absolutely in the hands of His power.

When we live by faith, we are constantly on the verge of the great spiritual world, because the power into which we have given everything is the power of the spiritual world. We are living, thinking and acting in constant recognition of the Supreme Power of the spirit, and are therefore constantly being touched by the spirit; and there is nothing that is more conducive to spiritual awakening than this tender touch of the spirit. To feel, through and through, that His presence is closer than breathing, nearer than hands and feet, is to arouse every spiritual element in our nature, and the soul will come forth into life clothed with the sublime glory of its own inherent divinity. Then we shall ascend into God's own beautiful world, and the life on the heights will begin.

When the soul discerns that My Father and I are One, the door to the kingdom of heaven within will be opened. To be with God is to be in heaven, and this is a privilege that any soul may enjoy now while yet in personal form.

To simply hope for health and freedom is to remain in our present condition however adverse that condition may be. But when we have faith in that power that can give us health and freedom we enter into the very life of that power, and we are healed at once. Faith moves on and on and enters directly into the very condition that is desired; it never ceases to press on until it is in the presence of that which is wanted, and therefore we can never fail. Hope stands on the outside; faith walks in; hope waits to be guided; faith trusts its own light and proceeds; hope waits for the right opportunity; faith creates its own opportunity; hope waits to see the solid rock appearing from out the seeming void; faith goes out upon the seeming void and finds the solid rock; hope stands upon the earth eagerly looking towards the heavens; faith mounts upon the wings of the spirit and ascends to the highest heavens.

CHAPTER XVIII

A Foretaste of Heaven

How to enter the silence is a problem that confronts every earnest seeker for that higher state of being, that more beautiful world of peace and joy, that inner realm where all is well, that secret place where dwells the soul with God. Prophets, illumined minds and great souls of every age have discovered that there exists a hidden somewhere in the cosmic life of man, the finding of which means the full realization of all the hopes of human life. In this inner realm there is healing for all ills, there is the peace that passeth understanding, the joy everlasting, and light, wisdom and power without end. To enter this sacred chamber of the soul is to find the answer to every prayer, the long sought fulfillment of every heart's desire; whatever the soul has longed for, the same will be found in this inner sanctuary of eternal life; and the path has been called the silence.

The will of the Father is to give us the kingdom; but we must go to Him if we would receive what is prepared for them that love Him. But how shall we go to God? We seem to be away from Him. There seems to be a gulf between our own life and the Infinite life. To bridge this gulf is the great need of the soul, and the silence seems to answer this need. Therefore, to know how to enter the silence becomes a great secret, both in the living of daily life and in the attainment of supreme spiritual life. To simply believe availeth nothing; we must actually go to God if we would receive what eternity holds in store. All things come from God, and he who enters into the presence of God will receive all that God can give. To go to God is to enter into the stillness of the spirit, into the silence of those secret places where the Infinite reigns in glory, where the Christ is enthroned On High.

Be still and know that I am God. This is the way, and no other path can be found. There are many who are trying to climb up some other way, but they will not find what they seek. The straight and narrow path alone leads to the Father's House. But there are few who find it, because the many try to reach the spirit without becoming spiritual. Man expects to gain the gifts of the spirit through methods, but never will he find the kingdom in this way. He alone receives the gifts of the spirit who becomes spiritual. He alone enters the kingdom who will live the life of the kingdom.

There are many who believe that psychical experiences constitute the "gates ajar" to the spiritual kingdom within, and multitudes have been lost in this sea of darkness and confusion. Such experiences never lead the soul to the kingdom, but they are, in many instances, the only obstacles in the way. So long as a person encourages those experiences and permits himself to be led by strange signs, he will remain in the without, and will suffer the usual ills of material man. The kingdom of heaven does not come by observation, neither tangible observations nor mysterious observations. The kingdom is found only in the spirit, and the spirit does not manifest itself in strange signs, but in the great and beautiful life. Jesus taught the existence of a spiritual realm within man, and emphasized again and again the necessity of living in this higher state if we would receive what real life can give. In this age, the entering of this secret place, the inner chamber of the soul, has been called the silence, or the true prayer of illumined faith—the prayer that not only asks of God but realizes eternal oneness with God. It is the prayer that is uttered in silence that is answered; it is the truth that is realized in the silence that gives freedom, peace and wholeness to man.

To enter the silence is to enter God's world, where everything is created in the image of God and manifests the likeness of God. To be in the silence is to know that you are spirit. To be in the silence is to know and feel that God is omnipresent and that you are one with God. To be in the silence is to actually be in the life eternal, and realize the divinity, the goodness and the perfection of all things. To enter the silence is to enter that sublime state where you know that God is in His Holy Temple and that all the world is silent before Him.

To enter the silence is not to have certain strange mental experiences for the space of a half an hour. You may have visions, you may realize the seeming reality of mystical realms, you may project thought, you may communicate with minds that are far away, you may have all kinds of super-physical sensations in mind and body; you may seemingly leave the form and be conscious of other worlds; you may imagine that your body is ether and that you can float upon the air; you may go into ecstacy and seem to receive wonderful revelations; you may have all of these experiences and many more, some of them real, some of them not, and never be in the silence for a single moment.

To enter the silence is to actually go to God; to enter into His presence and to know that He is ever with you. To enter the silence is to walk with God; to feel that His spirit protects you, leads you and keeps you, and that nothing but good can possibly come. To enter the silence is to awaken to the great truth that all that is real is good. To enter the silence is to become conscious of that cosmic state of existence where there is neither evil, sickness nor sin; where all is perfect and good; where life lacks nothing, and where the fullness of Infinite life reigns supremely through the all in all. To enter the silence is to see the soul-side of all things, to come face to face with the eternal, the changeless, the absolutely divine. In the silence you never look for experiences; you are above the world of experience; you are not in the presence of the passing; you are in the presence of the sublime stillness of that which ever and ever is as God is. When you are in a quiet state and have experiences you are not in the silence; but when passing thoughts are forgotten, and you find yourself face to face with the sublime stillness of eternal life, then you are in the silence. In that state all is silent and still; nothing is passing; all is; all is in Him; and all is illumined with the light and the glory of His radiant presence. Divine moments. Beautiful beyond human comprehension. A foretaste of heaven. A glimpse of the Many Mansions. Alone with God and the Great White Throne.

To enter the silence there are no special methods, but there are many things, which if done, will prepare the way. The first of these is to live the life of the spirit every day as far as you know; live in the spirit of the prayer without ceasing, and desire eternally the coming forth of the soul. And inspire this desire with the great truth that your soul is the throne of God. When the soul comes forth the Word becomes flesh, the perfection of divinity manifests in personal form, and the Mind that was in Christ Jesus the same Mind will be in you. Every day for a few moments be alone with the Most High. Let those moments be sacred, and think only of Him. Do not permit another thought to enter consciousness. Fill your being through and through with such strong spiritual aspirations that the thought of the Infinite reigns supremely in your mind. Try to realize His presence, His life and His love. Give yourself up wholly to God, and know that you are absolutely in His care. Enter so deeply into the spirit of this realization that you can actually feel divine nearness—that God is closer to you than your own life. To feel this is to enter into the greatest joy of sublime existence. To be touched by the Spirit of God, if but for a single moment, produces a million thrills of divine ecstacy, and so great is the joy that one short moment feels as if it were an eternity. In brief, when you are in that sublime state you are in real eternity; time passes no more; every moment appears to be an eternity because it is in eternity; and being in eternity it gives to you an eternity of bliss—unbounded bliss from the highest heaven.

There is nothing that will prepare the way to this sublime spiritual silence more than this—to give a few moments every day to God, to think of Him only, and to think of Him with your whole life, with your whole strength, with your whole mind, with your whole heart and with your whole soul. To give up to God is to enter into the kingdom of God, and to enter the kingdom of God is to receive everything that God has to give. To give up everything for God is to receive everything from God. To place everything in the hands of God is to be guided and led by the hands of God, and God leads man into every good that the mind can imagine. God leads out of the lesser into the greater, out of limitations into the richness of the boundless, out of mere existence into the glories and splendors of empyrean heights. And it is the purpose of the silence to so deepen the consciousness of the spiritual life that we may live eternally in the very presence of God. Thus we shall ever walk with God and be guided by Him in all things.

To consecrate your entire being to the spiritual life and so live that everything you do draws you higher and higher into the very world of the spirit—this is another essential to the attainment of the true silence. When your life is consecrated to the spirit, all the powers of your being will constantly ascend towards the supreme heights of the spirit. Thus you become more and more spiritual, and to be truly spiritual is to be able to enter the secret places at any time. Another important essential is to live in the consciousness of the divine side of all things. Never for a moment permit the mind to forget that there is a divine side to everything in existence. No matter how imperfect things may seem to be on the surface, know that there is another and a better side, even to the least of these; and do not for a moment lose sight of the great truth that that better side is created in His image and likeness. This lofty mode of thought and life will not interfere in the least with the duties of everyday life, but will instead make all work and all life a great joy. To work when the mind is in the spirit is to work both wisely and well; and when you ascend to the supreme heights of the spirit your work becomes a great work. To live in the spirit is not to live apart from visible things but to gain far greater mastery of things, and thus gain the power to do far greater things. To live in the silence is not to live in a dream; it is not to become oblivious to the realities of tangible existence but to inspire tangible existence with all the power, with all the life, with all the truth, and with all of the beautiful that the soul can find when it soars to celestial realms on high. The purpose of the silence is to unite the world of things with the world of spirit, and thus give the fairest life in all the world to body, mind and soul.

> Sun of my soul, eternal light,
> Be thou my leader and my guide.
> And I shall ever find the right
> By walking truly by thy side.
>
> Tho' clouds of doubt may hover near,
> Darkness and wrong obstruct my way,
> My faith in thee shall banish fear,
> And give my soul the light of day.
>
> Upward and onward I shall rise,
> Treading the path of truth and right,
> Passing through God's celestial skies,
> Led by the Spirit of His Light.

CHAPTER XIX

The Vision of the Soul

Faith is the "gates ajar" to the Holy City, to the world celestial, to the many mansions, to the spiritual realms, to the beautiful life, to the inexhaustible source of all that is good. Faith is the path that leads to the soul's inheritance of all that the heart has prayed for, and to follow this path is to have faith in faith.

Thousands have undertaken to live by faith, but not having sufficient faith in faith have too soon adopted a different course. In the beginning of the spiritual life it is so easy to forget the vision of the soul, so easy to follow the dictates of the senses when this vision has seemingly faded away. And the cause is we have not sufficient faith in faith.

When we begin to live by faith we must have sufficient faith to go on and on, no matter how many obstacles or failures we may meet at first. Temptations are numerous and the soul that has resolved to employ spiritual methods in all things must be able to deal with the tempter as Jesus did. But this is not impossible, because the mind that is in Christ Jesus, the same mind is in you.

The greatest obstacle is the intended kindness of friends. They have our welfare at heart and wish to do everything they can to promote that welfare; but they almost invariably employ the ways of the world; they do not know that faith is always sufficient. Here is a place where much strength is required. Here is the real parting of the ways, and the problem is, will you listen to those who love you with the love that knows not the way, or will you depend upon faith alone? Will you accept the kindness of the world or the unbounded love and the limitless power of the Infinite? Whoever loves brother or sister more than me is not worthy of me. Also, if thy right hand offend thee, cut it off. It is better to lose everything that is near and dear than to lose faith, but so long as we continue in faith, giving faith the first thought, and having abundant faith in faith, we shall not lose anything that we love.

The "right hand" is the sumtotal of all those things in the world that we feel we cannot get along without. They seem indispensable, and their loss seems irreparable; but they are insignificant compared with faith. We must be ready to dispense with them all if necessary to the realization of perfect faith, and we must depend absolutely upon faith regardless of the wishes of our dearest friends. But when we are ready to sacrifice everything that faith may have its way, we shall find that no sacrifice will be required of us.

When Abraham became absolutely willing to even sacrifice his own son in order to obey the spirit, he learned it was not required of him. And it is always thus; when we are willing to lose everything that spirit may reign, we find that we lose nothing but gain much.

When we have faith in faith we find that faith can do anything; and we find that faith in the life, the power and the guidance of the spirit will take us safely through anything. If we are in trouble, faith will open the way out; if we have lost our friends, faith will give us more and better friends; if we have lost all of our possessions, faith will give us greater riches than we ever had before.

We have been told that the story of Job is an allegory; but even so, it illustrates what can be done, and what is being done in varying degrees in the lives of thousands where faith in faith is abundant and strong. He who has the faith that Job had will regain all he has lost and in addition will receive much more. This is the law of faith and we can all prove the law by simply having faith in faith.

When we are in darkness and sin, faith will lead us into the full light; when we are in bondage to sickness and pain, faith will heal us and give us complete emancipation; and when we are in poverty or want, faith will lead us into the land of plenty.

The old thought has informed us that he who would live by faith must expect to live in poverty; many have believed this and have therefore been compelled to let go of almost everything of value and worth in the world. What we believe must come, will come. As your faith is, so shall it be unto you. If it is your faith that you must live in poverty in order to live by faith, in poverty you must live.

But it is the Father's will and desire to give us the riches of the kingdom; and to have faith is to live in harmony with Infinite will; therefore, when we begin to live by faith we shall leave the life of poverty and enter the world of abundance.

To live in poverty is not a mark of spirituality. If you are poor something is wrong either with you or with the society in which you live. But faith can take you out of that wrong and cause all things to become right. Faith can give you the best of everything that the whole of life can produce. Believe this and so it will be.

When things seem dark, and all that is near and dear seems to be slipping away from you, do not complain or weep. Have faith. Depend upon faith. Have faith in faith. Know that faith will change the course of events; turn darkness into light; turn hatred into love; turn chaos into order and harmony; and cause the best of all things to flow into your life in greater abundance than ever before. Faith can do anything. Have faith in faith and to you shall come the riches and blessings of the beautiful life.

The tendency of man is to turn to old methods when faith seems to fail; but why does faith ever fail? The reason is we have not sufficient faith in faith. When we have perfect faith in faith, it can never fail us. The power within faith is limitless, and it is our privilege to call into action as much of this power as we may need or desire.

We are called upon every day to decide upon something of importance; but how is this decision to be made? Are we to follow fear or faith? Fear declares that everything may go wrong; this is always the language of fear; but faith declares that everything will go right; and this is always the language of faith. Fear does not know; faith does know. Follow the verdict of fear and everything will go wrong, because the path of fear leads into wrong. But follow the superior insight of faith and everything will go right. The path of faith is the ever-ascending path to the greatest good that real life can give; therefore, no one can follow faith without finding the richer, the larger, the truer and the better.

Fear always expects the worst, because it can see only darkness; faith positively assures us of the best, because it can clearly see the light; and in the light the best is always found. But whether we decide to follow fear and live in darkness, or decide to follow faith and live in the light, will depend entirely upon how much faith we have in faith.

Millions are living lives that are not satisfactory; they long for a change, but they are in such complete bondage to fear that they are always afraid to even hope for something better. There is a power, however, that can break the bonds, and that power is faith. Are you living in Egypt? Are you in bondage to the king of evil, oppression and misery? Faith can lead you out. Depend upon faith, and begin this moment to follow wherever faith may go. Is there a Red Sea of mental materiality between yourself and the promised land of peace, happiness and plenty? Take the rod of faith in your hand and stretch it out over the sea; the waters will instantly divide, and you may walk safely to the other side. Faith can do anything. Have faith in faith.

There is not a single person in the world today that cannot enter the promised land, and do so now. Anyone may find peace, health, happiness, freedom, and the very best that life can give. These things are for you in your present state of existence. It is the will of God that life should be sweet to every soul; do not believe that you must suffer. There is freedom for you this very moment; there is a beautiful life that you may enter at once, and faith is the open door.

Have faith, and the veil of mystery is no more; you may see what has been hidden, and enter the secret chambers of life. Have faith, and the clouds of darkness will completely disappear; you will behold the light of the eternal sun, and the radiance of its glory will fill and illumine your entire sphere of existence. Have faith, and the barriers of limitations will fall to rise no more; and the invincible powers of the spirit will surge through and through your entire being, proclaiming in language divine, "Nothing shall be impossible unto thee, for I am thy strength and thy life forever."

Faith is the assurance of things hoped for, the evidence of things not seen; and the reason is that faith lives in the light. Faith knows that we may receive anything we ever hoped for, because faith discerns that power that makes all things possible. Faith is in the light, and therefore sees what has not been seen; it does not simply believe that the unseen is real, but proves the reality of everything by going out into the boundlessness of everything.

Faith is never sad, because it lives in the joy everlasting. Faith never grieves, because it knows that nothing is lost. Faith knows that what shall be united will be united; what shall be found will be found; and what belongs to us cannot long be kept away from us. Faith also knows that whatever we may need or desire now, exists for us now; and it is our privilege to enter through the door of faith and receive our own. The great secret is faith. Faith can do anything. Have faith in faith.

The soul never acts alone; whenever the soul acts, God acts also, in the same place, at the same time, and for the same purpose. Whenever the soul undertakes anything, there is immediate and direct assistance from the Supreme. Therefore, the soul can never fail; nor can any personal undertaking fail that is prompted, directed and inspired by the soul. My Father worketh and I work; and I am the soul. So long as I know and feel that I am the soul, the soul will act in all my work, and where the soul acts there God will act also, because the two are One. What the soul begins, God will finish; what the soul aspires to be, God will cause it to be.

CHAPTER XX

The Infinite Revealed

When we think of God as absolute and infinite, and try to picture His spirit as it fills the universe with His transcendental omnipresence, we seemingly lose, at first, that beautiful something that makes Him personal to us. God does not seem to be God unless we can think of Him as a friend, and go to Him as we would to some person that was very near and very dear. It seems difficult to speak to an Infinite Being, and there is no beauty or comfort in believing in God unless we can speak to Him at any time when we feel the need of His tender care. Nevertheless, our reason declares that God must be infinite or He would not be God; and our spiritual discernment concurs with reason upon this great, momentous theme; but since God is infinite, absolute and omnipresent, how can He be personal? And if He is not personal, how can we think of Him as being different from cold principle and law?

We cannot think of love as existing apart from personality, and God is love; therefore, He must be personal; but how can God, who fills the universe, be personal? This is the problem that confronts nearly every mind that passes from the literal belief in truth to the spiritual understanding of truth. When we try to think that God is not personal, we feel as if we have lost a great friend, the very friend of all friends; there seems to be no use for prayer, because how can the limitless Soul of the universe be interested specially in one of us, a mere atom in the immensity of the cosmos? Besides, we find it practically impossible to pray to something that is nothing but changeless principle and immutable law. We therefore cease prayer and substitute affirmations; but something is lacking; the soul remains comfortless; the intellect may be satisfied, but the tender elements of love and sympathy are gradually disappearing, and finally we come to a place where nothing but cold intellect remains. Then we discover we are not on the path; we have gone astray, and everything the heart has wished for seems to be far in the distance.

With God all things are possible; therefore, it is not beyond His power to be personal as well as absolute; nor is it beyond the power of man to understand how this can be. God is the great Soul of the universe. He lives and acts everywhere, and there is no place where He is not; nevertheless, He is just as personal to any one of us as the very dearest friend; in truth, more so, because His personal nearness to us is closer than that of any friend, closer even than life itself. He is not limited and circumscribed as the form of a human personality; if He were, He could be personal only to those who lived in the same locality as He might happen to live; and therefore the vast throngs would receive no more comfort from His personal care than if they should try to worship principle and law. The very fact that God is infinite makes it possible for Him to be personal to all the souls in the universe; and the fact that He is present everywhere throughout the limitless vastness of space makes it possible for Him to give His personal care everywhere, thus ministering individually to every soul in existence.

God is individualized in every soul; that is, He actually lives in the very being of every soul. God is within us, closer than breathing, nearer than hands and feet; therefore it is not necessary to look to the great Soul of the universe whenever we think of God, to look within is sufficient. To contemplate the vastness of infinite life or the immensity of a universal soul is to lose sight of God. We can know Him only when we meet Him face to face within the sacred realms of our own divine spirit. Do not look towards the vastness of the without, but look toward the divinity of the within, and God will be there. He is always there, and His being there means that He is personal to us, ever ready to give personal attention to any need that we may have at the time. Being within us, and being in the very life of our own spirit, He is nearer than even our own personality, and can therefore give us His personal attention whenever we may so desire. Though He is not personal to any one or any special number alone, being omnipresent, He is personal to all souls at all times, and that is a truth that is beautiful indeed to think of. The vine is united with all its branches, and gives its very life to each individual branch at all times. The vine is personal to each branch, and yet is not confined to the personal form or personal limitations of any one branch. In like manner, the Infinite is personal to every soul, but is not localized as any one individual soul may be.

When we state that God is in His heaven, we do not mean that He occupies a certain local heaven, because God is everywhere, and where He is there heaven must be also. Nor do we mean that He has a local throne, because the Infinite is enthroned in every soul, and all souls are spiritually one; therefore the great throne of God is the spirit of all souls united in one perfect, universal divinity. But there is also a local heaven; there is a local heaven in every soul, and God lives there eternally; there is a local heaven wherever two or more are gathered in His name; there is a local heaven wherever there is a new heaven and a new earth; there is a local heaven on the spiritual heights of every word of divine existence, and there are heavens above heavens both in the great without and the great within, the higher we ascend upon the great eternal path of endless and limitless glory. God has provided everything that the life of man may desire. There are heavens for the senses and heavens for the soul; there are heavens that the eye can see and the person enjoy, and there are heavens that only the soul can discern while on the mountain tops of its own exalted divinity. And everywhere there is God giving His personal thought to every human desire or need.

God is not a personality, but He is personal to every personality in existence. He is personal to each one of us because He is in actual personal touch with each one of us. He lives in all; therefore he is personal to all and can give personal attention to the needs of each and all. The soul knows this; the mind in its higher states of consciousness has discerned it, and thus the belief in a personal God has arisen. The mind has discerned only the personal presence of God in the soul at certain intervals, but the soul knows that God is personally present at all times in all souls. Thus the former belief in a personal God is not lost; it is only made infinitely larger. The feeling that we can speak to God as we speak to a personal friend continues, only that feeling has become infinitely more beautiful. To realize that God lives in us and we in Him is to know that we are personally in touch, not with a part of God but with all of God; and that all His power, all His wisdom and all His love is for each one of us now and eternally. All that the father hath is mine; and being infinite, He is personally interested in me even though He be personally interested in all the other souls in the universe at the same time. What He can be to one He can be to all, and He is. His eye is ever upon each one of us, and His hand is ever ready to guide whenever we may so desire.

God never ceases to think of you, nor should you cease to think of Him. He is personally interested in you and your welfare; then how can ill befall you? Why should any of us ever go wrong with the Infinite Hand so near? There are no reasons why unless it should be our endeavor to understand through reason that which the spirit alone can discern. Depend upon the spirit; follow the light of the spirit and every moment shall reveal the presence of God. Everything we do will be directed by His wisdom, and His power will see us through. Nothing need disturb us, neither need we ever be anxious. God wants us to reach our goal. He is personally interested in every undertaking we have in hand, and He is working with us, placing His limitless power at our command. Therefore, we need not be concerned when unexpected changes appear; every change will be a change for the better; every turn in events will lead us into greater events, and every door that may close on the left will open another door on the right through which we may pass to a greater world than we ever knew before. This is what will happen when God is with us; and He is always with us, only we must learn to receive everything that He has to give.

To know God is the beginning of wisdom, because God is the source of wisdom. The nearer we live to the source the more we receive of that which comes from the source. The mind that is not consciously living with God may have intellect and mental capacity, but the wisdom that knows can come only to that mind that is walking with God every moment of conscious existence. The mind that does not know God thinks in the darkness; the mind that does know God thinks in the light.

God is my light forever,
His spirit is shining within;
My home is the kingdom of heaven,
I'm free from all evil and sin.

God is my love and power,
My being is perfect and whole;
I'm living the life of the spirit,
The beautiful life of the soul.

God is my life eternal,
My truth and my wisdom divine,
I'm heir to His riches and glory,
His kingdom forever is mine.

CHAPTER XXI

Return Ye Unto God

Wherever we may be, whatever has happened or whatever may threaten to happen, it matters not; there is a power that can change everything. There are no reasons for sorrow, fear or regret; there are no occasions for anxiety, discouragement or despair; there is a path that leads to the world of the heart's desire, and anyone may find it. Great learning is not required, nor shall we find certain fixed beliefs necessary. The secret is simple, simple enough for any mind in the world, because it is the will of Infinite Love that every mind in the world shall know the way. None need stumble, none need go astray, none need ever be lost. All that is necessary is to follow the voice of the soul, and this voice is ever proclaiming in language divine, Return Ye Unto God.

The world has tried every imaginable method to gain freedom, but when all these methods fail, as they all will, Return Ye Unto God. The moment we return to Him, all that we have lost will return to us; and that which we do not wish for will vanish. When we return to Him we return to our own, because He is the source of everything that can possibly be our own. To be with Him is to be where we wish to be, and where we wish to be there we shall find the "gates ajar" to the heaven that is within. Before we can enter the heaven that is within us we must find perfect peace for mind and soul, and this peace we always find when we return to God. The more closely we live to His presence the deeper and more exalted the calm; and out from the silence of this calm comes the sacred symphonies of life, that music of the soul that we all recognize as the prelude to the kingdom of God. When we can hear it we know that His presence is near; we can discern through the spiritual vision those secret places that every returning soul has the privilege to enter. We learn what is in store, and life is not the same any more. We have had a vision, and all things have been glorified.

Return ye unto God. All other paths lead to sorrow and death, but in Him there is freedom and joy forever. In Him there is life, in Him there is peace, in Him there is wholeness and purity; in Him there is strength, in Him there is health, in Him there is power and truth; in Him there is all that life holds in store for man—all that the human heart can wish for. Seek no other source; follow no other path. There is only one place where the soul finds rest and contentment; only one place where every vision is realized, and every lofty dream made true. All may find it; the secret is simple. Return ye unto God.

But Jesus answered them,
My Father worketh even until now, and I work.
—JOHN 5:17.

The significance of this statement is as large as the limitless sea of divinity in which we live and move and have our being. The Infinite is everywhere and works everywhere, and therefore He is with us working with us. To know this is to know one of the greatest truths in the world, and there is nothing that is more helpful in the living of everyday life than to live, think and act in harmony with this truth. Whatever our work may be, it ceases to be difficult the moment we realize that God is working with us. When we know that His power is with us, the burden disappears completely.

The undertaking we have in mind may be very large; it may seem to be more than we alone can carry through; but we need not be alone; the Infinite is at hand ready to work with us, and with Him there can be no failure. Depend upon the Supreme; ask God to work with you; live so near to the Spirit that you will be one with God, and when you choose to go with God, He will go with you. Then the work will almost do itself; you perform the most difficult task with perfect ease, and you can work as much as you desire, weariness will not even make an attempt to enter your world.

The average person works alone; his task is therefore difficult; he does nothing well, and his work is wearing and tearing to a degree that makes his life both bitter and disappointing. But he works alone, with almost every disadvantage in his way, simply because he has not ascended in the spiritual scale. He has not arisen to that lofty realm where he can be in harmony with Supreme power, and therefore must depend upon the limited power of mere man. This, however, is his own choice; he may rise in the spiritual scale whenever he may desire and as much as he may desire; and the higher he goes in this scale the more direct assistance he receives from the Infinite.

When we reach those same spiritual heights that Jesus had reached, we can also say as he did that my Father worketh and I work, and we will receive just as much power from God as he received. We shall thereby do the works that he did, and as we go on still farther with him, we shall do the greater works. Jesus declared that he could of himself do nothing. His great power came from God, and his spirituality was so high that he could both receive and apply this power. He had reached that state where he was in perfect harmony with Supreme power and could manifest the fullness of that power in all his life and works.

And his command was: Follow me; what I have done, ye shall do. We are therefore not to remain content with simply believing that he was what he was and did what he did; we are to go and do likewise. Nor is the way difficult; to follow Christ is the simplest thing in the world, and there is nothing that produces such great results. Though we may not reach the heights that he reached at once, we can press on, and gain ground daily. Every step will bring added power, and this power we can use now in everything that we may be doing now. Spiritual power is not only for some other world; nor is its sole use in this world to keep us away from temptations. The power of the spirit is intended to be used in the living of a great life here and now and in the doing of great things in this present world.

Those alone will enter the kingdom who do the will of the Father, and to do the will of the Father is to live the life that He lives now. Live the life of the Spirit now, and you are saved both for time and eternity. And one of the greatest essentials in the living of the spiritual life is to live so near to God that His power is in everything that we may do. Then God works with us; not simply in what the world calls great things, but in all things. Even in those things that seem to be insignificant, the power of the Supreme is with us and everything we do brings joy.

The first step to be taken in anything we wish to do is to seek divine assistance. To ask God to go with us and work with us, and to enter into such perfect spiritual harmony with God that we can feel His supreme power through and through—that is the first and most important, be it work pertaining to body, mind or soul. Whether we are beginners in the spiritual life or have reached the heights, God will work with us in whatever we have the understanding to do now; and as we rise in the scale, He will work with us in doing those greater things that spiritual giants have the privilege to perform. And with God working with us, we shall never fail; all work will be pleasure, and the days of weariness shall come no more.

The mind that understands the spirit of truth knows that it is the Father that does the work; that it is the power of the Infinite that produces all power; that this power comes into our life to be directed and used by us, and that we may receive as much of this power as we desire. Such a mind knows that it will profit nothing to force the limited power that we may seem to possess, but that more power from on high comes without fail when our thoughts are very high and very still. Therefore, the true mind creates all thought in the supreme stillness of higher spiritual realms, and leaves results to divine law. Those results will be far greater and better than the personal man, unaided, could have possibly produced, even with every external advantage at hand. When we have great things to do we are tempted to rush forward and force those things through; but this must never be permitted. Such methods are not only detrimental to the mind, but are wholly inadequate to fulfill the purpose we have in view. To be perfectly still at such times and let Supreme Life do the great work is the secret.

To secure more power we must go up into those spiritual regions where power is limitless; and when we enter that high state our thoughts not only become enormously strong, but thinking becomes so smooth and easy that no effort whatever is required. We think God's thoughts after Him, and those thoughts are not only full of power, but also full of peace. To understand how an action can be perfectly still may be difficult to the mind that has never felt the perfect calm; but we must realize that stillness does not imply inactivity. Real stillness is the highest form of activity, where the strongest power acts in absolute harmony. To be in real stillness is to be in that power; therefore, the mind that is perfectly still thinks the highest thoughts, the greatest thought and the most powerful thought.

We may all demonstrate through personal experience that it is not strenuous metaphysical efforts that perform miracles, but the power of those high spiritual thoughts we create while in the secret places of the Most High. And when we learn to use that method only and never permit ourselves to become mentally overwrought, we shall develop healing powers that are extraordinary—powers that will do greater things than were ever seen upon earth before. "Greater things than these shall ye do." "I am with you always, even unto the end of the world."

When you live in the presence of the Infinite you are constantly in touch with higher power and superior guidance. You will therefore not only be able to accomplish far more in your chosen vocation, but you will be prevented from going astray. The very moment the person is tempted to take a misstep, the spirit from within interferes, and you are prompted to again proceed on the true path. When you are on the verge of doing something that is not best, higher power appears; something unexpected happens to upset all your proposed plans, and you are led to see, by the light from within, that there is something better in store. The nearer you live to the Infinite the more readily you are corrected and placed right whenever you are going to go wrong. Your seeming mistakes, therefore, are brought to naught in every instance, and you are awakened more and more to the realization of the great truth that God knows best. When in doubt or in darkness, leave it to God; the right way will open and the very best will come to pass.

The first principle in the unfoldment of the soul is to live in the spiritual attitude; that is, in the prayer without ceasing, or in that attitude where you feel that you are in the spirit. When you are in the spirit, or in the spirit of real prayer, and deeply desire certain things, you will certainly receive them. Everything that you can possibly pray for is in the spirit, and when you are in the spirit when you pray you will be in perfect spiritual touch with what you pray for. And what we spiritually touch, that we receive. Place human life in conscious contact with higher life and the latter will flow into the former. Soul unfoldment will place the being of man in higher and higher states of spiritual relationship with the Supreme Source of all things. Therefore, to unfold the soul is to open the way to every lofty goal that man may have in view.

"And if thy right hand cause thee to stumble, cut it off." The right hand symbolizes that which we think we cannot live without, and to think that anything in the visible world is indispensable is to be in bondage to things. He who knows that he can live whether the universe lives or not, has found life itself, the eternal life of the spirit. He is therefore no longer in bondage to things because he is in that life that is infinitely greater than all things.

CHAPTER XXII

Prayers That Are Answered

The Infinite is changeless; therefore there is no special providence in the usual sense of that term, and yet in the higher sense, everything is special providence. Every act of the Supreme is a special act because it provides for a special need somewhere in the life of the human soul.

However, it is not necessary to ask God to go outside of His changeless laws to answer our particular prayer. Our particular prayer is already provided for; that is, God is already doing that which is required to supply what we desire. Therefore, God will not have to do something special to answer our special request. He is already and eternally doing everything; but we must do something special to secure what God has already provided for us.

What is called special providence is not the result of a special act of God, but the result of a special act of man; and this special act of man is the act of man going to God to present his request and receive his heart's desire.

The prayers that are answered are not the prayers that we express when we are away from God, but when we are with God. Our prayers are never answered when we think of God as far away; to receive an answer to our prayer we must go to God; we must enter into His very presence, and while we are in His presence there is no true request that we can possibly make that will not be granted.

The Infinite is limitless, both in power and in love; therefore, God is not only able to do everything that we ask Him to do, but He wants to do it. It is a great privilege for infinite love to do everything, and the love of God is infinite.

It is not the wish of God to withhold from us anything that we may desire; it is His supreme desire to give us everything, but we are created with a free will; therefore God gives only that which we, through our own free will, may select.

The average person thinks he is imposing upon God when he asks for much; but the fact is that the more we ask for the more we please God, provided we go to Him and receive it, and if we wish to please God in the highest measure we should pray without ceasing, pray for everything we can use in the building of a great and beautiful life.

The power of prayer, however, should not be used exclusively for the realization of what is usually termed spiritual things; all things become spiritual when animated with the spiritual life; and all things are good when used for a good purpose; therefore, we are free to pray for everything that can add to the whole of life, be it of the body, the mind or the soul.

The true spiritual life does not mean the riches of the soul combined with weakness of the body, poverty of the person and ignorance of the mind. The true spiritual life is an ideal life on all planes, and God is ready to provide us with everything that can make the whole of life ideal, if we only pray for it with the prayer that not only asks of God but also takes us to God.

The true prayer never doubts, but believes implicitly that the request will be granted; and this is natural, because we cannot possibly doubt when we know that the more we ask of God the more we please God. But it is not only natural for the true prayer to have perfect faith; it is necessary. Before our prayers can be answered we must go to God and receive what we have asked for; and it is only through perfect faith in God that we can enter into the presence of God.

The true prayer is always inspired with the thought "I know that thou wilt answer me"; and this thought is the spiritual product of faith—the faith that feels the love of God.

The true prayer is also animated with the highest form of spiritual gratitude, and is therefore always inspired with that beautiful thought, "My Father, I thank thee that thou hearest my prayer, and I thank, thee that thou hearest me always." The prayer of faith knows that God does hear every prayer, and that He will answer every prayer providing we come to Him in person with our request. In consequence, when we are in the spirit of true prayer, our gratitude must necessarily be boundless.

When we feel that God will give us anything we may ask for, that there is no doubt about it whatever, we cannot otherwise but give expression to the very soul of gratitude, and this gratitude is both limitless and endless; it is the soul's eternal thanksgiving.

To live in the spirit of that prayer that is ever asking God for everything, that believes that God is giving everything, and that is constantly giving thanks to God for everything, is, in itself, a life of the highest joy. In such a life everything is being taken to higher ground, because we are manifesting in body, mind and soul, more and more of the likeness of God. Personal existence is becoming ideal existence, while the soul is living in the full conscious realization of God's own beautiful world.

> *But thou, when thou prayest, enter into thine inner chamber,*
> *and having shut thy door, pray to thy Father which is in secret,*
> *and thy Father which seeth in secret shall recompense thee.*
> —MAT. 6:6.

This is not a literal statement; the inner chamber is not some secluded place in some material structure, nor is the door referred to something that can be opened or closed with the power of physical hands.

There is only one inner chamber; there is only one secret place; there is only one sacred realm where the human meets the divine, and that is in the soul of man. To enter the inner chamber is to enter the beautiful stillness within. God is enthroned in every human soul, and to enter into the secret places of the soul is to meet Him face to face.

The door that must be closed is the consciousness of the without, that something in the mind that takes cognizance of the world of things. When we enter into secret, the visible must be forgotten; we are upon holy ground and must remove the shoes of external existence. We cannot enter the silent within so long as we think of outer things; therefore the door must be closed. And we cannot pray to the Most High unless we enter His presence. To pray is not simply asking God, it is also going to God. The most beautiful prayer is not uttered in words but is felt in the sacred depths of the soul.

When we simply ask God our prayers are never answered; we do not pray unless we enter into secret; it will profit nothing to make a request of the Infinite unless we first enter our inner chamber and close the door. And no person ever prayed in secret that was not rewarded openly. No prayer that is uttered in the sublime stillness of the soul is ever disregarded. All such prayers are answered. What we ask of God when we meet Him face to face, that we invariably receive.

When we have learned to pray in secret we should never have occasion to doubt any more. We then know that every request will be granted. Even though the answer does not come until the eleventh hour and the last moment of that hour, we know that it will come. Our faith is as perfect as the word of truth, and as high as the heavens of the spirit, and in that faith we live. God will find a way; we have asked Him to do so and every request brings that beautiful response, "I will not forsake thee nor leave thee; I am thy Redeemer, I will care for thee."

To enter the inner chamber of the soul is to transcend everything, for the time being, that pertains to the visible world; but this requires spirituality. We cannot enter the spirit so long as we are subject to the body, and we are subject to the body so long as we live for the body. When we begin to live for the spirit we can enter the innermost chambers of the spirit whenever we so desire, and when we are in this spiritual state we may pray for anything that is needed in the body, the mind or the soul. What we pray for in secret we shall receive openly. Therefore, to live for the body is to neglect the body and to lose the soul. But to live for the spirit is to give the fullness of life to the entire being of man.

When we pray openly we do not pray, because we cannot be in the secret chambers of the soul so long as we are in the material world of external things; and no desire is a prayer unless it is uttered in that secret place within where we meet Him face to face. We must be with God to receive of God, and as He is enthroned within us, the perfect path to His presence is to enter the spiritual chamber within. There we shall find, not only the sublime stillness of the soul's communion with God, but also the secret power of faith—the faith that makes all things possible.

The secret power of faith is found in the soul's nearness to God; the nearer we are to God the more perfect our faith, the greater our power and the more beautiful our life; and when we enter into the sacred realms of the soul we are in the very presence of God. We are touched by the spirit, and to be touched by the spirit is to be filled with the spirit—to be filled with everything that the perfection of divine spirit may contain.

The prayer without ceasing is the living of that life that is so near to God that we can feel His power and His love at all times. In that life the mind is in constant touch with the soul and every true desire becomes a prayer uttered in secret. Therefore, when we so live that life itself becomes a beautiful prayer, there is nothing that we can desire or ask for that we shall not receive. When we live so near to God that we actually have our being in the spirit of His life, our every desire will be just and wholesome and true, and all such desires will be fulfilled; not in the distant future, but now. We shall begin to receive now that which is in store for them that love Him and every day the measure will increase as long as eternity shall continue to be.

> *If ye abide in me, and my words abide in you,*
> *ask whatsoever ye will, and it shall be done unto you.*
> —JOHN 15:7.

There is no stronger statement to be found anywhere in the literature of the world, and there is possibly no statement that has received less attention. Nevertheless, those who understand the inner meaning of high spiritual truth know that this statement is not only based upon an exact scientific principle, but that any spiritually minded person can demonstrate the whole truth that is contained in that principle.

To abide in the Christ is not simply to live in the acceptance of some belief about Jesus, but this is the current idea and being purely literal it has no power whatever; in consequence, those who claim to abide in the Christ do not secure any greater results through their prayers than do those who depend solely upon mere personal desire. To abide in the Christ is to actually live in the Christ consciousness, and every part of mind and soul is permeated, through and through, with the life and the power of the Christ. Your entire being is in the hands of higher power; you are in a world where things are absolutely mastered by the spiritual will, and your mind is so spiritualized that it responds perfectly to the power of divine will.

When the words of the Christ abide in you, your mind is in absolute truth because those words are absolute truth. The mind that is in truth is in the true state of being, and to be in the true state of being is to be so close to God that anything desired can be received at any time. With God all things are possible, and God will do anything for us if we live as He lives. This is the secret, and we do live as God lives when we abide in the Christ with His words abiding in us.

When the words of the Christ abide in us, every thought we think and every word we utter will be animated with the spirit of the Christ; in like manner, inner spiritual power will give soul to everything we do, and that power that caused even the winds and the waves to obey will begin to work through us. Supreme power will be with us at all times to answer our prayers; our thoughts and our words will be living thoughts and words, and will carry the power of the spirit wherever they may go. We are therefore in that position where we not only can receive from God anything desired, but where we have the power to make our own prayers come true.

To be in the Christ means more than to receive from his love what our hearts may desire; it means spiritual mastership. To be in the Christ is not a mere feeling of the emotions; it is a life, and in that life the power of the Christ is supreme. Nor is this power given to us temporarily; it becomes our own, and we become able to bring to ourselves anything we may ask for. It is the promise. "What I have done, ye shall do." This promise is not mere words; it means something; it means that any person may attain spiritual mastership and cause the world of things to respond to the power of the Christ within him.

We have believed this; the hour is at hand to prove it and those who will try will find that God is with them. But we must remember that this supreme state does not come through personal effort. "I can of myself do nothing." We must enter the consciousness of the Christ, the inner life of the Christ, the very spirit of the Christ; and our thought must become identical with His word. When there is no difference whatever between our thoughts and the sublime words of the Christ, then we can truthfully say that His words are abiding in us.

When our thoughts become identical with the words of the Christ, the same power that was in His words will be in our thoughts and also in our words—a principle of truth so extraordinary that when we first think of it we become awe-stricken with thoughts so great, so wonderful, so marvelous that no tongue can ever give them utterance. And as we penetrate further into the inner meaning of this great truth we meet thoughts more marvelous still; we are face to face with the statement that we, even we, shall in the near future hold in our own hands the same power that wrought such wondrous works in the hands of the Christ. Every person that is living the spiritual life is steadily moving toward that supreme goal.

When we abide in the Christ and His words abide in us, we are living absolutely in the inner spiritual world; in that world there are no impossibilities, and everything that we can possibly ask for is even now at hand; that all our prayers should be answered is therefore most evident. God is more willing to give than we are to receive; the reason why we do not receive what we may desire or need is because we are not willing; that is, our will is not in harmony with the will of God and our desire is not in harmony with the desire of God. But this harmony with God is fully secured when we begin to live in the Christ and begin to think only those thoughts that are inspired by the words of the Christ. We are then absolutely in His power, in His life, in His love; we may ask what we will; His life contains everything; His power brings forth everything; His love gives everything.

> *Therefore I say unto you,*
> *all things whatsoever ye pray and ask for,*
> *believe that ye have received them,*
> *and ye shall have them.*
> —MARK 11:24.

This great statement gives positive emphasis to the law that we can gain actual possession only of that which we have gained conscious possession. Or, in other words, we must become conscious of the existence of an object before we can gain personal possession of that object. We must enter consciously into the life of that which we desire to gain, but we cannot enter into the life of that which we doubt the existence of. Doubt invariably produces a gulf between ourselves and the object of doubt, while faith produces mental and spiritual unity.

Spiritual unity is always followed by actual or personal unity; that is, what we enter into conscious possession of in the spiritual life we will, ere long, gain actual possession of in the physical life. Believe that you have already received in the spirit what you desire to receive in the person, and you will receive it in the person in a very short time. This is a law that positively cannot fail. Claim your own in the ideal world and you will receive your own in the real world.

This law gives rise to the practice of affirmations, but affirmations as usually employed do not comply with all the elements of the law. To simply affirm that we are what we wish to be or that we have what we wish to possess, is not sufficient. Our spiritual possessions do not express themselves unless there is a strong, positive, personal desire for expression. We must pray for that which we wish to realize, but our prayer should not be mere asking. The prayer that asks in the feeling of uncertainty as to whether the thing prayed for is for us or not, is not a prayer of faith; and it is only the prayer of faith that is answered.

To pray in the feeling that knows that what we pray for is, even now, ready to be given to us, is to combine the desire for expression with the realization of possession, and we thus comply fully with the law of supply. In this attitude we have faith, and it is only through faith that we can enter into the spirit of that which we desire to actually possess. We must awaken the spiritual cause before we can secure the physical effect, but it is only through faith that we enter into the world of spiritual cause. Faith produces spiritual unity, and when we are one with the spirit we become conscious of the life, the richness and the power of the spirit. In consequence, we cause that which is in the spirit to be brought forth in the body, because what we gain consciousness of in the within we invariably express in the without.

When we simply affirm that we have what we wish to possess, the mental action is quite liable to be merely intellectual or even mechanical; and we do not touch our interior, spiritual possessions in the least. But when the affirmation is animated with prayer and desire, the mental action becomes so deep that the spiritual life is reached. Or, to express the same truth in another manner, when our prayer for that which we desire is strengthened by the positive faith that we have already received it, we remove all doubts and barriers and enter at once into actual and conscious possession.

To use affirmations alone is to ignore the great possibilities of Infinite assistance. Any person may, for a while, build himself up mentally and personally with affirmations alone, but the structure is artificial; it is built upon the sand and will surely fall when the storms of environments and changing circumstances become a trifle too strong. Without the conscious and continuous assistance of the Infinite no man can travel very far on the upward path nor go very high in the scale of true being. But any man who takes God with him can overcome any obstacle in the world, scale the highest heights in existence, and what he builds today he is building for eternity.

The proper course to pursue is to ask God for everything you desire; ask Him to be with you in everything you wish to accomplish; pray without ceasing, and while you pray and work and press on to the great goal you have in view, affirm with positive faith that God is with you, that He has given you everything you can possibly desire or need. Believe that you have what you pray for, believe that you are what you wish to become; then ask God to enlarge your realization, to give perpetual increase to your faith, and to be constantly with you in working out these great supreme convictions.

The true prayer is a high spiritual communion with God, but it is not an inactive state. True prayer is oneness with God and a strong living desire for the full realization of all that is in the life of God. Therefore, the true prayer is the perfect way to God. If we wish to be with God we must pray. If we wish God to be with us we must pray. Live in constant prayer to God and you secure the constant and conscious assistance of God in everything you do. But a prayer is not a prayer unless it incorporates the affirmation of the truth upon which the prayer or desire is based.

To simply affirm that God is with you will not give you the assistance of God. When you affirm a truth you are talking to yourself; when you pray you are talking to God, and God listens only to what we say to Him. If we want God to go with us we must ask Him; we must talk to Him consciously if we wish His personal assistance and power.

To affirm the truth is absolutely necessary because affirmations will train our own minds in right thinking, will remove doubt and will develop in us the power to know that all that we can pray for or desire is ours now. But in order to enter into the actual realization of our own we must enter the kingdom of God, because all things that are in store for man are now in the kingdom. And it is true prayer—the prayer that goes to God—

that constitutes the "gates ajar" to the riches and glory" of that wonderful kingdom.

> *And Jesus lifted up his eyes, and said, Father, I thank thee that thou heardest me. And I know that thou hearest me always.*
> —JOHN 11:41.

This beautiful statement was given before the answer to the prayer was received and is therefore an illustration of the very highest form of supreme faith. To thank God after you have received what you asked for is simple; any heart can, at such a time, be full of sublime gratitude, but to thank God before you have received what you intend to ask for, and feel the fullness of that gratitude thrill every fibre in your entire being—that is spirituality indeed. Likewise, to be able to say that you know that God hears you always; only the mind that is in the spirit can make such a statement and pray in this manner, but that alone is real prayer.

To precede any prayer with doubt is to close the door between yourself and the spirit; there must be no uncertainty in our communion with God; we do not believe that God is God so long as we are uncertain as to whether our prayers will be heard or not and we cannot enter into the presence of God until we believe that He verily is God. When we know that the power of God, the wisdom of God, the love of God—all is limitless, we can feel no doubt whatever, as to whether or not our prayers will be answered. Divine power can do anything, but divine love cannot refuse anything.

When we know God as He is, we know that He hearest us always, and we feel it a privilege to thank Him every moment for this great truth. And when we thank Him in this manner before we begin our prayer, we not only enter into the very love of His spirit, but we also enter into that faith that makes all things possible. The faith that knows that God hearest us always is so close to God that it is animated with the very power of God; and therefore when we are in such a faith nothing can be impossible; we may then ask for what we will and it will be done unto us.

The more perfectly we realize that God hears us always the higher we ascend in the scale of true spirituality, because this supreme faith lifts the soul higher and higher until we are received at the very throne of the Most High. And to be in His presence is to receive whatever we may have asked or prayed for. God is everywhere, and we may enter into His presence anywhere. The Most High is enthroned in every soul, and pure spiritual faith is the "gates ajar" to His beautiful kingdom.

There is abundance of hope in the world, but what we need is more faith. Everybody is hoping for better things; the poor hope to get rich; the sick hope to get well; the sad hope to gain happiness; the troubled hope to find peace; everybody is hoping for something, but few have the faith that is necessary to secure that something. When we are in bondage, or keenly realize our bondage, we hope that the Great Deliverer will come; we pray that He may come; we hope that our prayers will be answered, and we are so absorbed in our hopes that we fail to hear Him knocking at the door even now. To have hope is to face the door, but hope stands still; it never moves toward the door. To live in hope is simply to face the great goal, but we may continue to face that goal for ages, and never move forward a step. "To live in hope is to die in despair," because hope remains stationary; it never gains what it hopes to gain. But when faith begins we remain stationary no more. We press on directly, and with power, towards the coveted goal; our hopes are soon realized; our desires are granted; what we wished for is withheld no more; through faith we have entered that world where every prayer is answered and every wish made true.

CHAPTER XXIII

The Faith That Moves Mountains

To him who has faith nothing is impossible. It matters not what he may wish to realize or what he may wish to do; if he has faith, it can be done. But what do we mean by faith? Faith is not a passive belief; it is a positive action. It is the power of the spirit within man acting upon the life, the mind, the body and the nature of man; and by acting through man it acts upon everything with which man may come in contact. When we have faith we do not simply believe in the form, or that which may exist in the external; when we have faith we enter into the spirit of that in which we express our faith; the secret of real faith and the real power of such at faith is therefore found in the spirit.

When you proceed with something you wish to accomplish, do not simply have confidence in yourself; and do not simply proceed in the mere conviction or assurance that your purpose will be realized; do more than that; have faith, and when you have faith, your mind will enter into the very spirit of that which you have undertaken to accomplish. This is the reason why nothing is impossible when you have faith, because when you enter the spirit you enter the power of the spirit, and to the power of the spirit there is no limit whatever. To have faith is to enter into the spirit; to enter into the spirit is to enter into the life and the power of the Most High; and with God all things are possible. The entire world of things is permeated with spirit, with infinite power; therefore, when we enter into the spirit of anything we enter in the one spirit that lives in all things and gain possession of as much of the power of the one spirit as we can possibly receive. The greater our faith the greater our capacity to receive of the limitless power of the spirit, and in consequence the greater will be our realization of whatever we now may have in view.

To have more and more faith, the secret is to enter more and more deeply into the spirit of everything in which we express our faith. Do you have faith in yourself? Then try to enter mentally into the spirit of your entire being whenever you think of yourself. Do you have faith in your work? Then try to enter into the spirit of everything that is connected with your work. Do you have faith in every person you meet? Then try to enter into the spirit of his life, into mental contact with the greater man that lives within the personal man. Do you have faith in all things? Then enter into the spirit of things, into the real soul of things whenever you think of things or look upon things. Do you have faith in God? Then enter mentally and spiritually into the spirit of Infinite Spirit whenever you think of God; whenever you think of God, think of yourself as being in the spirit of God and try to feel that God is closer than breathing, nearer than hands and feet. The more deeply, the more fully and the more completely you enter into the spirit of that of which you think, the greater your faith; and the greater your faith the greater your power.

There is not a person in the world who may not proceed in life with the full conviction that his ideals will be realized and that he will accomplish everything he has undertaken to do. If he lives and works in faith he simply cannot fail, because faith will give him all the power he may require, and anything may be accomplished when we have sufficient power. But the average person proceeds in the thought that he may possibly reach his goal; he is not certain; he concludes he will try, and will do his best; but as to the outcome he does not know. This, however, is not faith, and without faith nothing whatever can be accomplished. To fulfill any purpose, even the most insignificant, there must be some measure of faith, and the greater this measure, the greater will be the realization desired. He who proceeds in real, unbounded faith will place his life in touch with invincible spirit, and he will continue unmoved, untouched and undisturbed, no matter what the circumstances may be. He will place his mental vision upon the highest light of supreme faith, and whatever may happen he will never waver from that light for a moment. He will continue with ceaseless perseverance and the most positive determination; he will continue in faith, and as he continues and grows in faith he will gain more and more power until he has sufficient power to do everything he is determined to do.

Faith does not always produce the expected miracle at once; it does not always convert a life of confusion, sickness and failure into a life of happiness, harmony and abundance without much waiting and watching and prayer; it does not always change a pathway of thorns into one of roses the very first day we begin to live by faith; and it does not always remove every obstacle in a minute. There are times when it requires months and even years of constant faith to realize what we pray for; but we may rest assured in the great truth that whoever fixes his attention upon a certain definite goal and continues to work towards that goal in faith will positively reach it.

Work in faith, in continuous faith, in the spirit of unbounded faith, and you will reach your goal, you will accomplish your purpose just as surely as the coming of another day. Therefore, though you may not have results at once, nor even for some time, continue to work in the same unbounded faith; the results you desire will positively be gained; and the deeper and stronger your faith the sooner you will reach the object in view.

When faith seems to fail, the remedy is more faith. Do not become discouraged in the midst of seeming failure; do not give up the purpose you have undertaken to fulfill; do not doubt the possibilities of this purpose, nor come to the conclusion you are moving in the wrong direction. Continue to work in more and more faith, and if you should be on the wrong path, something will happen to set you right. Enter more and more into the light of faith, and all things will clear up. When you are on the wrong track, doubt and uncertainty will but confuse you more and cause you to go further into the wrong. But faith will increase your light; faith illumines the mind and clears the sky of your entire world; faith will lead you out of your mistakes and give you enough power to regain all that is lost and more. Continue, in faith, to press on towards your goal; discord will soon become harmony; uncertainty will soon become positive convictions; the crooked will be straightened out; obstacles will disappear; you will find your proper place; you will enter the work that is intended for you; all things in your life will work together for good, and you will press on and on, gaining ground steadily, drawing nearer and nearer toward the highest goal that your spiritual vision can possibly discern.

The majority of minds have many obstacles to meet and almost invariably give emphasis to the belief that every seeming obstacle actually is an obstacle; but faith does not look upon obstacles as obstacles; faith does not call difficulties difficulties. When a person begins to live in faith, all things that come into his life are looked upon as opportunities, and they are. We all know very well that if we had no difficulties or obstacles to meet, or what would be more appropriately termed "great occasions," we should soon become nonentities. It is the difficult things that we meet that enable us to bring into action the greater power that is within us; difficulties, therefore, are the most valued of opportunities, and if taken advantage of as such, will always be met with joy. No obstacle should ever be called by that name or ever thought of as being an obstacle, for it is, in truth, something that will enable you to prove to yourself that the power that is within you is greater than anything in the world. When we no longer call obstacles obstacles or difficulties difficulties, we shall not be disturbed by obstacles or difficulties any more. Whatever we meet will be turned to good account and will call forth more and more of the greater power that is within us. Accordingly, all things will work together for greater good; every occasion will be welcome, no matter what it may be; every experience will be a pleasure, and everything that we pass through will add to our welfare and joy.

When a person thinks that every obstacle is an obstacle, he will frequently hesitate to proceed; and will, in many instances, on account of this hesitancy or doubt or fear, fail to reach his goal; but if he proceeds in the faith that there is something within him that is greater than all the obstacles in the world, there is no obstacle that can stand in his way. In fact, when he proceeds in such a faith, every obstacle that is met will simply call forth that greater something that is within him, and this "something" will give him all the power he may require to reach his goal.

Faith is that attitude of mind through which we come in conscious touch with the Infinite. When we are in the attitude of faith we are in the very spirit of life, and in the spirit of life God reigns supremely. The power of the Infinite is in the spirit, and when we are in the spirit we become one with that power; therefore, while we are in that oneness nothing can be impossible with us any more. But the power of the Infinite, expressed through us while we are in the spirit of faith, is not applicable to spiritual things alone; it is applicable to all things, and may be applied anywhere in life in the attainment of the higher, the greater and the better. If you wish to change your environment, or if you wish to better certain things in your life, determine precisely what you want; then have faith. Continue to say, "I have the faith," and repeat that statement as frequently as possible. Believe that you will realize what you want and believe that your belief is absolute truth. Have faith, and also have faith in faith; and whenever you affirm the statement, " I have the faith," enter into the very spirit of that statement. When you say that you have the faith and enter into the spirit of what you say, you awaken the power that can do what your faith has undertaken to do. That is how faith can never fail; the moment you begin to have faith in what you have undertaken to do you arouse all the power necessary to see that undertaking through. And the more frequently you affirm, in the spirit, "I have the faith," the sooner you will enter into the spirit of real faith, where the necessary power will be gained.

Our constant purpose should be to become conscious of the inner spirit of faith; and when we feel this inner spirit we should try to become conscious of the still deeper spirit that is within our first realization of the spirit. To go deeper and deeper into the realization of the spirit should be the ruling desire whenever we enter the attitude of faith; and as there is no end to the depth or the height of the spirit, there is no limit to that inner world of life, wisdom and power that may be realized through faith. However far we may enter into the spirit we can always go farther still; every step that we take in spiritual realization opens the door to a still higher spiritual realization, and whenever we proceed, through faith, to enter more deeply into the limitless spirit of faith, we open another door to the marvelous kingdom within. Faith goes into what seems to be unreality and finds that the deeper we enter the world of the spirit, the more real and the more substantial the spirit becomes. Faith goes out upon the seeming void and finds that there is no void; all is real, and the farther we go out into the vastness of limitless life the more real and the more beautiful life becomes. Therefore, to follow faith is always to pass from the lesser into the greater, into the better, the richer, the larger, the more wonderful and the more beautiful.

The mind that lives in doubt can see limitations everywhere; the mind that lives in faith can see no limitations, and, in fact, knows that there are no limitations anywhere. The mind that lives in doubt is in bondage to these seeming limitations and therefore realizes nothing more of life than what is confined within these seeming limitations; but the mind that lives in faith lives in the freedom of the all of life, and is daily realizing more and more of everything that is contained in the all of life. Faith can see that no matter how large or how beautiful life may be now, there is always a larger and a more beautiful life to live for, to work for and to realize in the days that are near at hand. In the life of faith there is no end to anything; there is always something more, always something richer, always something greater, always something better. The life of faith is therefore full of realization, full of promise, full of joy. What was promised by faith yesterday is realized today, because faith is not only the power to see the greater vision, but is also the power that can lead life into the very world of the greater vision; and thus the promise of yesterday is always fulfilled today.

Every person in the world, whatever his present position may be, can begin today, and through the power of faith work himself up into any attainment or realization he may have in mind. Whatever his goal, he can reach it, if he works in faith. This may seem to be a strong statement, but Jesus Christ declared it was so; and it is certainly high time that we begin to believe and practice the great truths this Master Mind proclaimed. If the teachings of Jesus mean anything they mean that I can, through faith, overcome anything in my life, change anything in my life, better anything in my life, and realize any goal whatever to which I may aspire to reach in life. Though it may take months and years to reach certain things, those things that have exceptional worth, nevertheless I can do it, if I continue persistently to work in the spirit of unbounded faith. And, in the meantime, if I give this same faith to all my work, I shall be gaining ground daily, making my life larger, better, richer and more beautiful constantly. When I begin to work in the spirit of faith, I will always be in touch with the spirit; and to be in touch with the spirit is to be at one with God, because the kingdom of God is in the spirit; therefore, when I am in the spirit, I am with God; God is with me; God is on my side, and we two constitute a majority; we are greater than anything we shall ever meet, and we have the power to do anything we may desire, to work out anything, accomplish anything or realize anything that we may at any time have in view. Faith has made us one—the Infinite and myself—and together we hold, not simply the balance of power, but all power. Therefore, knowing this to be true, why should I ever doubt any more; why should I ever hesitate any more; why should I ever be fearful or afraid any more.

There are thousands of richly endowed minds in the world that accomplish nothing to speak of and the reason is they live in the confusion of doubt, uncertainty and fear. Many of these minds would become giants in the world if all their powers were spurred to action by the invincible spirit of faith. In fact, there is not a single mind, whether naturally endowed or not, that would not come forth into a larger, richer life if inspired by the wonder-working power of faith. Faith awakens the all that is in human life and makes that all a continuous power for good. Therefore, not a person in the world, whatever his work may be, can afford to live or work a single moment without faith, without the deepest, strongest faith that he can possibly arouse in his own soul. Faith is not for the spiritual world alone, but for every world. Not a muscle should move unless it moves in faith; not a thought should be formed unless it is filled with the spirit of faith; not a word should be uttered unless it comes directly from the limitless power of faith. This is what it means to live by faith, and such a life is a life indeed.

There is a belief among many that since every soul has the power to draw upon the limitless for any desired supply, it is not necessary to give special attention to physical or mental efforts. In other words, if they continue to live in faith they will receive what they want; their own will come, even though they be very inefficient as far as work is concerned. This is their spiritual theory, but it is a theory which, when applied, leads invariably into poverty both of body and mind. The fact that "all things are yours" on account of your divine heirshi; and the fact that your spiritual nature is actually and permanently one with the limitless source of every good thing in existence, does not prove that you may receive all that you need by simply declaring, "My own cannot remain away from me." To fold your hands and wait in faith for your own to come is not to wait in faith; hope stands and waits, but faith goes to work. Therefore, if you are waiting in faith you have no faith; and having no faith you will continue to wait; your own will not come. In the real, "all things are yours," but you can make no actual use of the riches of the kingdom within until they are brought forth into manifestation. The life, the power and the riches from within, however, will not manifest through a mind and body that is dormant; and the habit of waiting and hoping for supply to come, regardless of efficient personal effort, has a tendency to make the faculties and the elements of the human system more or less dormant.

To have faith is not simply to believe that everything will come to us or that everything must come to us because everything already belongs to us. Faith is not simply belief; it is an attitude of mind and soul wherein you place your own life in perfect contact with infinite life; and, in consequence, when you live and work in faith every thought and every effort will be charged, so to speak, with the power of infinite life. To work in faith is to give more life and more power to your work; to think in faith is to animate and inspire your thought with a finer insight and a higher degree of understanding than you could ever receive in any other manner. The mission of faith, therefore, in practical life, is to give the individual that greater measure of wisdom and power through which he may make himself worthy of the very highest good that he may desire as his own. All things belong to us; that is, all things are ready for us whenever we can use them; but we cannot use the greater things in life so long as we are living a small, partially dormant life. The riches of the kingdom are not for us "to have and to hold"; they are for us to use and we can use them all only as we become alive with the life more abundant in every element of body, mind and soul.

The principle is this: Use the body, use the mind, use the soul, use every faculty, use every force, use every power that you can possibly find and arouse throughout your entire being; and use all these things in faith; that is, while you are using all these things, place your life, your mind and your consciousness in such perfect touch with the Supreme Source of life, power, wisdom and inspiration, that you become a perfect channel of expression for all that is great and worthy in the vastness of sublime existence. In this manner, you become so worthy, so competent and so efficient in your life that all that is great and worthy in the ideal can be naturally attracted and used by you in the real.

With regard to this subject, the human family divides itself into three classes. The first class is composed of the masses of men and women in the world, those who try to live and try to accomplish something in life by depending solely upon objective faculties. They proceed without paying any attention to the greater powers within them or to their relationship with infinite life; in consequence, they are constantly hemmed in by their own self-created limitations, and as a rule, merely exist. The second class is composed of those who go to the other extreme, depending almost entirely upon the power of the spirit to provide supply, while the true and full use of the powers of the personal man are either wholly or partially neglected. These people are buoyed up in the beginning with hopes and expectations, and for a time their spiritual theory of life seems to work; but ere long they find themselves drifting into adversity and want, and are forced to return to the ways of the world, as mere existence is better than annihilation. The third class is composed of those who combine the powers of the personal man with the powers of the spiritual man; they make a special effort to turn all their powers and faculties to practical use, and to all their work they invariably add the inspiring attitude of unbounded faith. The members of this class try to develop all their faculties to the very highest degree; they try to place body, mind and soul in the best working condition; they try constantly to increase their working capacity because they are not only believers, but doers; they are disciples of work, work that adds to the welfare of the world, and they always work in faith; they try to make the best use of everything in their possession, but while trying to push to the front, so to speak, the best that is in them, they try constantly to develop a higher and a finer conscious realization of the great truth that we live and move and have our being in the limitless power of the Supreme.

That all the great men and women that have appeared in the history of the world have come forth from this last mentioned class is most evident; and that no person can ever rise in the scale of life unless he applies the method of this class is equally evident. To depend solely upon the personal man is to merely exist; to depend solely upon the spiritual man is to be a dreamer, not a doer; but when the powers of the personal man are combined harmoniously and practically with the powers of the spiritual man, we cannot only dream; we can also make our dreams come true. What we discern in the ideal we can cause to come true in the real. We provide practical working capacity on the personal side and limitless power on the spiritual side; whatever we may wish to do, attain or accomplish in the great without, we may receive all the wisdom, all the understanding and all the power required from the great within. We shall thus demonstrate the great truth that "all that the Father hath is mine," not simply for spiritual contemplation, but for actual, personal possession and use in the tangible world today.

That the powers of the spiritual man can be readily combined with the powers of the personal man in the producing of practical results is a fact that is constantly being demonstrated in the lives of thousands. We all know of remarkable instances where people have, when in the midst of extreme want, sickness or despair, placed themselves in the hands of higher power and secured emancipation under circumstances that have seemed miraculous. Many a person has found himself in a position where everything was lost, where all the elements were against him, and where not a single ray of light could be found anywhere; but by placing himself in touch with the power of the Supreme, and by going to work in full conscious oneness with that power, has caused everything to change in his favor. Many a person has demonstrated the great truth that by taking God with him in his work, he could overcome every obstacle, remove every barrier, vanquish every enemy, disperse everything that was against him, and come out victorious under circumstances that, in the beginning, seemed utterly hopeless. It has been demonstrated thousands of times that where the personal man alone was helpless, complete emancipation and victory were made possible where the powers of the spiritual man were combined with the efforts of the personal man. This is therefore a principle that no person can afford to ignore, no matter what his work may be.

Whatever we may wish to do or gain, there must be personal effort; but the more perfectly we are conscious of the limitless powers of the spirit within us, the greater will the results of those efforts be. And this is not true of certain special efforts alone; it is true of all efforts from the least significant on the physical plane to the most important on the sublime cosmic plane. It is true, not only in instances of man's extremity, but also in every state or degree of man's prosperity. If the power of the spirit, when combined with personal effort, can take man from death's door into perfect health, as has been done thousands of times, even when all hope was lost and every other method had failed; and if this same power, when combined with practical work, can take man out of the lowest depths of adversity, poverty and despair, and place him on the very heights of freedom, power and limitless supply, is there any reason why the power of the spirit cannot be combined with personal effort in all the affairs of everyday life and thus give an ever-increasing measure of health, happiness and prosperity to man? Man calls upon God when everything else has failed; but he should call upon God before he tries anything else, and he would never fail.

Though we may be strong physically now, and be in possession of exceptional capabilities and advantages, we cannot afford to ignore the fact for a moment that increase comes only from the within. "They that wait upon the Lord shall renew their strength"; none others. The present strength of the body will not hold out unless it is constantly replenished from on high. The present capabilites of the mind will shortly lose their brilliancy and power unless they are kept in the highest state of perfection through constant contact with the light and the life of the soul. It is not wisdom to use up the limited powers of the person and utterly ignore the great interior source of inexhaustible power. Yet man does this very thing; therefore, his person is weak, his days are short, and his life but a trifle better than mere existence. There is, however, a better way; let the powers of the spiritual man be constantly combined with the life, the powers and the efforts of the personal man, then shall the person of man never be weak; his days may be lengthened indefinitely, and his life will become richer, more beautiful and more inspiring, until a million joys are blended harmoniously in every moment of his endless existence.

We are all heirs to the kingdom, not only the spiritual kingdom but the entire kingdom of life; we can receive, however, only what we can use; we need only what we can use, therefore to receive more at any time would be superfluous, and there is no place for the superfluous in the realms of divine law. There are many that can use much, very much, but the majority do not receive as much as they can use because they do not live and work in the consciousness of the "all things are yours." Others receive but little at any time because they do not fully use what they already possess. We draw upon the universal for greater supply in proportion as we turn to good account our present supply; though we must remember that no person can turn to good account the best that is in him now unless the efforts of the personal man are filled through and through with the powers of the spiritual man. The work that we do in faith is the only good work and the faith that we apply in work is the only true faith.

The average person thinks that it is his privilege to continue to "hold" his possessions, regardless of use, and that he can accumulate as much as he likes; but this is not true. The true life is not lived for the purpose of accumulating things. Many have realized this and have gone to the other extreme, concluding that the only true life was the life that had no tangible possessions whatever. There are only a few, however, who have taken the path that lies directly between these two extremes, And that is one reason why the power of the spirit to combine with the power of the person in practical life has not been as extensively demonstrated as we should wish. But it is our privilege to demonstrate the true law of complete existence; and when we do, the reward will be great indeed.

Every individual is entitled to all the riches of the spiritual kingdom, and in addition, to the possession of as many things, and as beautiful things, in the visible kingdom, as we can possibly appreciate and use in the enrichment of all the realms of his own entire existence. But before he can secure all these things, he must cause his personal nature and his spiritual nature to live together and work together as one. He must work for everything that he may desire, and must work in the faith that every desire will be fulfilled.

To express the law of this principle more briefly, the first essential is to make the best use possible of everything that we may possess now. The second essential is to live, think and work in faith. He who lives in faith lives in the spirit, and he who lives in the spirit lives in God. No person can afford to do anything without taking God with him; no person can afford to think a single thought without realizing that that thought is created in the infinite sea of divine thought; no person can afford to express a single desire without realizing that that desire is the expression of some supreme, some great, some beautiful state of interior existence.

It is extremely important to try, as much as possible and as frequently as possible, to enter into the inner consciousness of the great truth that "all things are yours." As we grow in this consciousness we actually enter into real, limitless possession; and when we begin to "inwardly feel" that we possess the rich and the beautiful in limitless supply, we will begin to attract the rich and the beautiful from every source in the world.

Take the statement, "All that the Father hath is mine," and mentally dwell upon the very innermost truth that can be found in this statement. Try to realize what it means to possess everything that there is in the kingdom of the Infinite, and enter into the very soul of that meaning. Try to feel the spirit of limitless, divine possession, and resolve to live perpetually in the innermost life of that spirit. The consciousness of limitless supply will soon become an actual factor in mind; and we can begin to draw upon the limitless when we are actually conscious of the limitless.

When you actually realize that "all things are yours," you will never be anxious about the future any more. You know that there will be a ready way to supply every need at the proper time. You do not live in the possession of simply the barest necessities; you live in the life of abundance, and the rich and the beautiful in your life is constantly on the increase. But you are never disturbed about the greater needs that you know will come in the future. You live in the positive faith that when the greater needs are at hand, the greater supply will also be at hand. And your faith always comes true.

To live in this faith is to live in perfect peace; we are never disturbed about any threatening circumstance; we are never fearful or afraid any more; we know that the door will open when the time comes; we shall surely have what we need—enough to supply the greatest possible need. Having done our part we know that God will not fail in His; for as much greater is His faithfulness than ours as the entire cosmos is greater than a single drop in the sea. "I will not forsake thee nor leave thee"; upon this we may always depend.

When you look into the future, do not be anxious about methods or means to carry out what the future moment may demand. When you come to that place, God will be there; the limitless powers of infinite life will be there; the wisdom, the light and the luminous understanding of your highest spiritual nature will be there; all of you will be there, and the power of your faith to draw upon the limitless for any desire or need will also be there. Then why be fearful any more. Why be anxious about anything. All things are yours now, and the now that now is, is eternal.

Though your bark may be tempest-tossed, be not alarmed. The Christ is asleep in the ship. You may call Him at any time; and when you do the heavens will be cleared, and a beautiful stillness will come over the vastness of the deep. What does it matter to you what may threaten in days to be; the Christ will always be with you; wherever you may choose to sail upon the infinite sea of life, the Christ will always be in your ship. For lo, I am with you always. Whether He be asleep or awake, where you are, there He will be also. You may call upon Him as you will, and peace shall reign supremely in your life once more. For the winds and the waves shall obey my will. Then why be fearful or afraid any more. He can still any storm in the world, and bring the silence of the heavenly calm wherever His presence may be.

CHAPTER XXIV

The Winds and the Waves Shall Obey My Will

Then he arose and rebuked the winds and the sea;
and there was a great calm.
But the men marveled, saying, what manner of man is
this that even the winds and the sea obey him.
—MAT. 8: 23-27.

We all come to places at times when the sea of life is tempest tossed, and the winds of adversity are mercilessly raging about us; we are all placed in circumstances at times when everything seems to go wrong, when everything seems to be against us, and when we fear lest we perish; but at such moments we should remember that the Christ is in the ship. No matter what the ship of life may be; no matter what manner of men may be sailing in that ship, or what their purpose may be, wherever man may be found sailing upon the sea of human existence there the Christ will be found also. Wherever we may be or wherever we may go, the Christ is in the ship. "For, lo, I am with you always." And it is our privilege, under every circumstance, to awaken the Christ. When we do, he comes forth invariably, and the winds and the waves will obey.

Whenever we enter into that higher and more sublime state of being where we meet him face to face, the consciousness of the Christ within us is awakened; we are in the Christ state; we are in the presence of Supreme Power; we are at one with God; and upon us comes a beautiful calm. The winds and the waves in our own minds are stilled, and upon the great sea of thought within us the billows are tossing no more; the storm has ceased; the black clouds have disappeared; all is beautiful and still; and the peaceful waters seem radiant with joy as they glitter in the sunbeams from the smile of God. We have opened our minds and souls to the strong and peaceful presence from on high; thus we have placed ourselves in the beautiful calm; and when we are stilled, all that is about us will be stilled also. As man is in the within, so will his life be in the without. When he can still the storms of his own mind he can also still the storms of adversity in his outer life. It matters not what is taking place in our own circumstances, all must change when we change; all must be stilled when we are stilled; and whenever we awaken the consciousness of the Christ within, upon us comes a beautiful calm.

When we know that the Christ is within at all times; when we know that whenever we call upon the Christ to come forth, the winds and the waves will obey; and when we know that the very hour the Christ is awakened, everything in life will be stilled, harmony will come out of everything, peace will come out of everything, and good will come out of everything. When we positively know this, need we have any fear whatever concerning the future? Need we fear opposing circumstances or adversity? Need we fear any condition that might arise? Nothing can happen that need disturb us in the least. The Christ is always in the ship; we may call upon him at any time; he will never fail to come forth, and when he does, there will be a great calm; peace will reign once more, and all will be well again.

Those who do not know that the Christ is in the ship are living constantly in fear; they reason that almost anything might happen to place obstacles in their way, or that certain conditions might arise to upset everything they had undertaken to do; and the things they fear usually come upon them; but when they know that there is a power within that can be awakened at any time—a power that is greater than anything in the world—fear may be banished for all time. When this great truth is realized we need never be concerned about the future any more, and anxious thought may be banished forever; whatever may happen in the future there is a power within that can change anything as we may desire, and turn anything to good account as we may desire. We may thus live in the conviction that all things will work together for good, for greater and greater good, and we may know that this conviction is based upon nothing less than eternal truth.

The Christ is always in the ship, always in every ship that may pass upon the sea of life; and he may seem to be asleep; we may not be aware of his presence within us, but our unconsciousness of his presence does not prove that he is asleep, or that he is never there. The Christ is never asleep. The only begotten son of God that is within all, within everything, that is the ruling power in every soul, the Supreme I Am in every soul, is never asleep. The statement that the Christ was asleep in the ship is metaphorical. It is not the Christ that is asleep, but our own consciousness of the Christ. When our own consciousness of the Christ is asleep we are not aware of his presence, and he seems to be asleep to us. When we are not aware of this great spiritual power within us, we are unconscious of that power; we are asleep, so to speak, as far as the existence of that power is concerned, and therefore will never think of awakening that power. But when we have attained sufficient spiritual discernment to know the power of the spirit in our own soul, we shall begin to call forth that power. From that moment higher power will be with us, and we shall no longer be victims of the tempest tossed sea; whenever the billows begin to toes or the storms begin to rage, we may call forth the Christ; he will always be with us, and will always respond to the call; he will answer our prayer with his own presence, and in his presence all is beautiful and still.

This same unconsciousness of the presence of the Christ within also explains the seeming loss of the soul. The soul is the Christ individualized, created in the image of God, and therefore can never be lost. The soul is co-existent with God, always is with God, and that which is eternally with God can never be lost. But the personal man is sometimes so engulfed in materiality that all view of the soul is lost. The soul is always there within us, ever abiding in the shining glory of the kingdom of God within us; the soul is safe, always was safe and always will be safe, safe in the life eternal; but if we are living in materiality, we do not see the soul, we do not feel the soul, we are utterly unconscious of the soul and therefore conclude that there is no soul. Or, if we are sufficiently awakened to feel the soul, but not sufficiently developed in spiritual discernment to know the divine nature of the soul, we may conclude that the soul is weak and imperfect as the flesh, and that it may go down into pain, bondage and misery at any time, now or in the future. And thus has arisen the seeming need of the doctrine of future salvation for the soul. Such a doctrine, however, is not based upon the spiritual conception of the soul, but was formed when we looked upon the soul through the confusion of materiality. The soul is never lost, never can be lost; and as you are the soul, you can never be lost.

The soul is always safe with God, therefore you are always safe with God Realize this truth, and you will find the soul; you will find that you are identical with the soul and that all is well with the soul now as all is well with God now.

To save the soul is not to save the soul, because the soul needs no salvation, but to restore the power of the soul as the supreme ruling power in your whole life. Enthrone the soul in every thought and action and you save the soul, not from sin, because it is free from sin, but you save the soul from your own personal neglect. The power of the soul is no longer neglected but is saved for actual use in the realization of health, freedom and mastery throughout your entire being; thus you gain emancipation for every element in your being, and that is the salvation we seek. We are saved in the true sense of the term when the divine power of the soul reigns so completely throughout the mind and the body that all the ills of life are completely banished from mind and body. We are saved in the true sense of the term when the body is filled with the power of health and wholeness, when the mind is illumined with the light of eternal truth, and when the soul is abiding forever in the splendors of the cosmic realms. And such a salvation is realized when we no longer ignore the soul, but place the soul upon the throne of being as complete master of everything that we may ever think or do or say. To enthrone the soul, the principle is to follow, not the desires or the tendencies of the person, but the supreme purpose of the spirit, and to depend absolutely upon the power of the soul in all things, knowing that the power of the soul can see you through no matter what your life, your work or your purpose may be.

The belief of the many is that whatever we may wish to accomplish we must depend wholly upon ourselves; and that we must depend upon ourselves as far as our ability and power may go is very true, but it is not true that we should depend "wholly" upon ourselves. We can receive power and aid from sources that are above the personal self; and what is equally true, no one ever scaled the heights in life that did not depend constantly upon these higher sources. The best ideas, the noblest thoughts and the greatest truths that have ever appeared in the world, came to man when his mind was in the upper regions, in touch with the spirit sublime; and the power with which all great things have been wrought, has come from the same source. Men and women who depend wholly upon themselves, their personal selves, are weaklings; they come and go without doing anything aside from sustaining existence; but men and women who depend upon Supreme Power as well as their own ability to work out their purpose in harmony with that Power, invariably become giants in mind and soul. It is the deeds of such minds that become lights on the path to greater things; it is the lives of such souls that reveal to the race what true spiritual existence has in store; and it is the work of such men and women that has given us the light, the freedom and the happiness that we now enjoy.

You may live in absolute darkness today; you may not know where to turn; your sky may be black and a raging storm may be almost upon you; you can see nothing but destruction as you have no idea what to do; you are about to give up and perish, but as this thought passes through your mind you remember the "last resort"; you remember the great statement: Call upon me and I will answer thee. You then call upon that power that should be sought first, but that men usually seek last when in trouble. You turn to the Christ that is asleep in the ship. You open your mind to light and power from above, and almost at once there is a rift in the cloud. You are in absolute darkness no more, and the threatening storm is beginning to "break." You pass more completely into the spirit of the Christ, and you realize the beautiful calm. The clouds are gone; you are in the light; you can see everything clearly, and you know what to do. You are now in touch with that upper region from which you may receive better ideas, greater thoughts and more valuable truths than you ever received before; in consequence, you will find precisely what you may need in securing emancipation from external adversity, and in building for those greater things that alone can satisfy the aspirations of the soul.

The belief that the Christ within can still the winds and the waves of every condition that we may meet in life, and change every circumstance into one of calmness, harmony and well-being, is a truth that can be taken into every event of daily life. No matter what may come; no matter what the obstacle or the difficulty may be, there is something within us that is greater than anything in the world. The Christ is with us in the ship; we may call him at any time; he can still any storm, change any circumstance and remove every obstacle that we shall ever meet. His power is not applicable to conditions of mind and soul alone, but to physical conditions and circumstances as well. There is nothing that will not respond to the ruling will of the Christ within, and there is no place in practical life where the power of this will may not be applied to the greatest advantage. He who lives in constant touch with Supreme Power is always in possession of the most power, and he may apply this added power in body, mind and soul. "They that wait upon the Lord shall reenew their strength"; but this added strength does not simply appear in the spirit; it appears also in the mind and the body.

Therefore, it is always profitable to be in touch with Supreme Power, and to depend upon Supreme Power, whether our work be physical, mental or spiritual. It is not wisdom to depend solely upon the lesser things of the person when we may constantly receive power and aid and inspiration from the greater things of the spirit. All things are for man; and the use of all things should ever be his purpose, no matter what his work may be.

We have found a perfect remedy for fear, because he who knows that the Christ is always in the ship will fear nothing. To him no ill can come whatever. Though the approaching storm may sweep everything before it, its fury will be dissipated into nothing when it comes to the ship where the Christ is awake. But the Christ is in every ship, and he will come forth in every ship and utterly put to naught the impending danger. Whatever our position in life may be, or whatever we may be called upon to do, when we know that the Christ is with us we may proceed calmly, peacefully and serenely in the full conviction that nothing but good will come. We need fear nothing because there will be nothing to fear. The turning of the tide may sometimes be delayed until the eleventh hour, and even until the fifty-ninth minute of that hour; but the turn will come without fail. We may continue positively in that faith. "I will not forsake thee or leave thee." This is the truth, and we can, under every circumstance, demonstrate this truth, providing we never fail to call the Christ. We must go to the Christ first; then he will come to us and answer our prayer whatever that prayer may be. We must place ourselves in touch with Supreme Power first; then that power will come with us; and when Supreme Power is with us we have nothing to fear. When the power of the Supreme is on our side all things will be on our side; and God will go with us the very moment we choose to go with God.

When the day is calm, it is well; but if it is not calm, it is also well; it will soon become calm if you call upon the Christ, for "the winds and the waves shall obey my will." If the future seems bright, you may rejoice; but if the future seems dark, as dark as the blackest night, you may also rejoice; there is a power within you that can put adversity to flight and turn misfortune and sorrow into the glory of a cloudless day. When all that is good is coming into your life you may be grateful; but when all that is good is passing out of your life you may also be grateful; the Christ that is within you cannot only save your ship from every threatening storm and impending danger, but he can also guide your ship toward the shores of richer treasures and greater good than you ever knew before. Grieve not when in the midst of loss; rejoice with great joy, and be grateful from the deepest depth of your heart. Call upon the Christ and you will regain everything and more. There never was and never will be any real occasion for disappointment or tears; when the lesser disappears, turn to the greater; you will find the gates ajar, and you may enter at once into pastures green.

The power of that will that causes the winds and the waves to obey comes invariably from the depths of spiritual existence. It is the power of the Christ enthroned in the soul, and whoever will recognize and call forth the reigning Christ within will gain possession of such a will. But we can never gain such a will so long as we try to dominate the lives of others or try to forcefully control external circumstances or events. Nor can we gain such a will so long as we try to will with the outer mind. The real will comes from the great spiritual depths of being, and as it is coming forth it causes the being of man to become deeply calm and enormously strong. The difference beetween the man of real will power and the man of mere external force is readily discerned. When you meet the latter you find a great deal of domineering effort expressed through the most superficial of action; but you find the man, himself, weak and easily overcome by almost any adverse condition; when you meet the former, however, you will find yourself in the presence of a truly strong man, a man who is strong and alive all the way through to the very depths of his inexhaustible being, a man who is actually conscious of irresistible power; and you inwardly know that such a man cannot be moved by any power in the world; he has gained possession of that something that is greater than anything in the world, and wherever he may journey upon the sea of life, the winds and the waves must obey.

To depend exclusively upon the personality of Jesus and that power of the Christ that manifested through him twenty centuries ago, is to ignore the present power of the Christ within us. Thousands are doing this, and, in consequence, continue in sickness, trouble and sorrow. To depend upon any personality, no matter how sacred or how highly developed, is to depend upon the outer form and ignore the interior spirit. Such a practice leads into materiality away from spirituality, and materiality means bondage. To follow the Christ is not to worship the person of Jesus but to follow absolutely the light and the spirit of the Christ in your own soul today, The power that can calm the waves on every tempest-tossed sea does not come through any external personality; such a power can come only through the great spiritual depths of your own soul or, to state it differently, from those sublime spiritual heights within where the Christ reigns eternally. When we follow the Christ that is here today, the Christ that reigns in the spiritual kingdom within today, we shall steadily grow in spirituality, emancipating mind and body from every form of bondage and from every condition of materiality, until that freedom that comes from the truth divine has been realized in its greatest measure. Then we may also say, My yoke is easy and my burden is light. Then we may also speak the great word, Peace, Be Still, and to us shall come the beautiful calm.

> Rock of Ages, truth divine,
> Strong foundation, ever mine;
> Safe, secure, I here remain,
> Free from evil, sin and pain;
> Living ever in the right;
> Fixed on high with souls of light.
>
> On the rock of truth I stand,
> Destiny at my command;
> Filled with power from on high,
> Boundless good forever nigh;
> Far above the world of wrong,
> Safe with truth, so firm and strong.
>
> Every height in truth's domain,
> I shall reach and thus obtain
> Every wish within my heart
> For no blessing can depart;
> All of good is ever mine,
> On the rock of truth divine.

CHAPTER XXV

For I Have Overcome the World

These things have I spoken unto you,
that in me ye may have peace.
In the world ye have tribulation: but be of good cheer;
I have overcome the world.
—John 16:33.

There are two distinct worlds open to man in his present state of existence; in the one he finds tribulation; in the other he finds peace; the first is material; the other is spiritual, and it is man's privilege to choose which one he would have as his present place of abode. If he selects the material, he sacrifices everything that has real value in life; he secures a few fleeting pleasures and much pain; not a single moment gives real satisfaction, and nothing that he can do produces the results expected.

But when he selects the spiritual, he sacrifices nothing that is good; he secures all the joy that life can give; his pains are few, if any, and when they do come, they come to lift him higher; every moment is rich, every hour is thoroughly worth living, and there are many periods of time when his soul is lifted to the supreme ecstasies of the highest heavens; whatever he does he builds wiser than he knew, and he not only receives everything expected, but more.

Therefore, those who understand what the spiritual life holds in store, may be of good cheer; their sorrows and tribulations are over; better days are at hand; the words of the Christ have prepared the way, and that way leads to peace. No matter what external conditions may be; no matter what circumstances we may be in now; we may be of good cheer. "I have overcome the world"; and in Him we may live whenever we so desire. The power of the Christ can overcome anything and change anything, and that power is in us. Then why should we not rejoice, and rejoice in Him alway?

There is something within us that is greater than things, and it is our privilege to claim the power of that something now. "I have overcome the world now, and every soul may live in Me now." That means emancipation now for all who will receive it. Freedom is not for some other world, but for the life we are living today. We are not required to live in tribulation at any time during present existence; the way to complete emancipation is before us at all times. I am the way. Whoever will transcend personal consciousness and enter into the consciousness of I Am will enter that life that is not of this world, and he will gain that power that can overcome anything that may exist in this world.

To enter the supreme life of the Christ is to gain the supreme power of the Christ; and to steadily grow in the consciousness of that life and power is to rise out of every tribulation until complete emancipation has been gained. That supreme life is in store for us; it already exists in the supreme I Am of our own being; this I Am is the Son of God, the only begotten of God, the

Christ in us; and the Christ that is in each one of us is one with each one of us. That is how "I am in the Father, and ye in me."

This supreme oneness wherein the soul is one with the Son and the Son is one with the Father, is real; it is not merely in thought or in feeling; it is not solely an abstract state of being; it is as real and as tangible as life itself, and every element that pertains to that oneness is as real and as tangible as life itself. I am the way, and you are that I Am; you must be or you could not be one with the Father. If you are not that I Am you would be separated from God, and no soul can be separate from God and live. Claim your divine sonship; claim your divine inheritance; claim that supreme power that overcomes the world; it belongs to you; it is you; know this truth and this truth shall make you free.

To believe that you are a mere, weak human being is not to be in the Christ; when you live in the Christ you are filled through and through, with supreme power and you know neither weakness nor tribulation any more. This is evidence that you are in the Christ. When you live in Him you are stronger than any adversity that is in the world; you remain untouched, unmoved and undisturbed no matter what may threaten in the world; you are in Him and in Him you have found peace. You have entered the spiritual world, and I Am the door to that world; you have risen to that supreme state of being where you can say, in the spirit of eternal truth, I Am, and through the power of that truth you have overcome the world.

The attitude of overcoming is usually thought of as being inseparably connected with resistance, and as being directly antagonistic, in its action, toward that which is to be overcome. Nearly every person, when trying to overcome anything, begins to resist, begins to antagonize, begins to work against that which is not desired. Accordingly, he does not succeed because he must work in the opposite direction before his purpose can be fulfilled. The first principle in overcoming is to give no thought whatever to that which is not desired. The more completely we can forget that which we wish to overcome, the better. The second principle is to give our whole attention to that something which we know we shall realize when we have overcome. If a person is in adversity he knows that when this adversity is overcome certain most desirable conditions will be realized. Then let him begin at once to give his whole attention to those desirable conditions. By giving his whole time, thought and energy to the attainment of that which is desired, he will invariably overcome and rise out of that which is not desired. We overcome the wrong by turning completely away from the wrong, and giving all our life and power to the greater realization of the right. This is the secret of overcoming.

When we devote all the power of thought, all the power of soul, all the power of life to the constant attainment of greater and better things, we shall ascend perpetually in the scale of existence. This means perpetual growth and, in consequence, the elimination of evil, because all evil is caused by retarded growth. The purpose of life is to move upward and onward forever; to live is to live more; but no person is actually living more unless he is living more every single moment. The moment he begins to live more he begins to ascend, and when he begins to grow into the greater he begins to grow out of the lesser. When he grows into the right he grows out of the wrong; he gains freedom from that which is not desired by entering more fully into the life and the spirit of that which is desired. But the moment he ceases to live more, he retards his growth; he violates the purpose of his life, and instead of supplying more life he supplies less life; his real nature, however, demands more and more life, and therefore, demand and supply will at once become unequal. There will, accordingly, be a lack of something in his life, and every evil that man has ever met came originally from a lack of something. Real life demands the living of more and more life; but when man fails to live more and more, the natural demand in life will not be fully supplied; the lack of one or more things in human existence will be the result, and conditions of evil invariably follow.

Real life is lived in the individuality, the soul, or the real man; and so long as we consciously live in the real man, or in the I Am of being we shall continue to live more and more. We shall thus realize the fullness of life constantly and constantly grow into a larger measure of that fullness. Life will be full; there will be no lack of life and no retarded growth in life; in consequence, there will be no evil in life; we shall have perfect freedom and there will be nothing to overcome. Accordingly, we shall fully comply with the great statement, the true way to overcome is to so live that there is nothing to overcome. However, when we do not consciously live in the individuality, or in the real man, but live consciously in the personality only, we are not in touch with the constantly ascending current of real life; we are not in touch with that greater measure of life that will enable us to live more and more life. A lack of life will at once be felt, and here we have the original cause of every ill, every wrong and every undesirable condition that man can know. This is the real fall; conscious living falling down from the living of unlimited life in the individuality to the living of limited life in the personality. But this fall did not take place only once ages ago; it is taking place every day in nearly every mind, and is taking place many times a day in most minds. To be saved from this fall, which is the only fall, proceed to live in the spirit, in the soul, in the real life of the I Am of being. Express the life more abundant in the personality, but live in the individuality. By living consciously and constantly in the individuality you will live in the life more abundant. You will live the limitless life, and what we live we express. We express in the personal man whatever we live in the real man; and therefore when we live the limitless life in the real man we express the limitless in the personal man; thus the personality is ever filled with the life more abundant; there will be no lack of life anywhere in the being of man; and there can be no evil where there is no lack of life.

To try to remove or overcome evil is nothing but wasted effort; evil is not a thing but a condition arising from a lack of life. When necessary life is supplied, there will be no further lack of life, and where there is no lack of life there can be no evil. To antagonize evil, to resist evil, to work against evil will not remove evil. Supply the life more abundant and evil will disappear of itself. Evil is simply emptiness, and no place can be empty when every place is full. To supply the life more abundant, live in the soul, in the real man. Do not establish yourself in the personality; establish yourself in the individuality and live in the source of life instead of in the partial manifestation of life. This is the simple secret. Go up into more life and you overcome everything that is not desirable in life. Do not try to overcome anything; simply begin to live more. Give no thought to evil; never try to remove evil; give all your thought to the attainment of the good, and direct all your effort towards the attainment of an ever-increasing measure of good. When you see evil, do not become indifferent; proceed at once to add to the good; when the good is on the increase evil is on the decrease; this is invariably the law; and the good will begin to increase the moment we begin to live more.

The same principle should be applied in every thought, action or relation in human life. We should never emphasize or ever recognize that which is not desired; but that which is desired should be recognized constantly and be emphasized most positively at every opportunity. When we meet others, their imperfections and shortcomings should be overlooked, while their good qualities should be given special attention. When we think of ourselves we should apply the same rule, and we should apply it universally in all physical, mental and spiritual training. The child that is trained in this manner from birth will naturally become extraordinary. When all the power that a person may possess is employed in the building of greater things, there must be great results, even though the power originally possessed be limited. The average person, however, employs but a fraction of his power in the upbuilding process; the remainder is employed in resisting evil and adversity. The reason why we are not higher in the scale of life, and not more perfectly developed in body, mind and soul, is because we have emphasized our imperfections, and have failed to give our good qualities special attention. You give your life to that which you emphasize; therefore give no thought to weakness or imperfection; give all your thought to those desirable qualities that you wish to build up; your worthy qualities will soon become so strong that weakness can no longer exist in your nature. Build up what you want; that is how you overcome and remove what you do not want. The more fully we can concentrate the whole of attention upon that which we desire, the sooner it will be realized; and when that which is desired is realized, that which is not desired can exist no more; therefore give all your thought, all your power, all your life, and the whole of your attention to that which is desired; do not try to remove the lesser but work uninterruptedly for the greater. The lesser is left further and further in the rear as you approach the greater goal that lies before you.

The process of overcoming is an ascending process, with the eye fixed upon the eternal mountaintops of spiritual supremacy. Give constant recognition to the very highest states of spiritual supremacy that you can possibly discern, and desire all the elements of your being to move perpetually towards those sublime states. You thus produce this ascending process; you will begin to grow out of, to rise out of everything that you have wished to overcome; and when this ascending process has been placed in full, continuous action, there will be nothing further to overcome. The wrongs that we wish to overcome have been produced by retarded growth, but when we are ever rising into more and more life, growth will no longer be retarded; and, in consequence, there will be no further wrongs to overcome. It is therefore evident that if you are still meeting things to overcome, you have not learned to live more and more; you are still permitting yourself to fall down from the world of real life into the world of temporary conditions; you are still living in the body instead of manifesting in the body; and you are still following the confused desires of the personal man, when the only true desire can arise in the real man. To go up into more life, into the limitless life of eternal being, is the remedy.

Whenever you find yourself in any adverse condietion, remember you will not come out of it until you grow out of it. You may antagonize adversity and cause it to disappear temporarily, but it will soon return in some other form. Nothing, therefore, is ever gained by such a method. Train yourself to grow out of that which is not good by constantly growing into the greater good; and we invariably grow into that which we think of the most. Think constantly of that which you desire, and you will grow into it. But your thought must be of the heart; it must be deep and strong, and inspired by the invincible power of soul. Do not give personal force to your thought but try to feel that every thought you think has soul, and know that every thought that has soul has the power to do whatever it was created to do. And in all your efforts to grow into the better, the greater and the more beautiful, consider the lilies of the field; grow like the flowers and you will never fail. The flower resists nothing, antagonizes nothing, works against nothing; it gently comes out of its gross and earthly environment, and grows on peacefully, silently and serenely until it becomes an inspiration to all the world. Human life can do the same, must do the same, if we wish to realize the life beautiful and become conscious of the richness and glory of the spiritual heights.

Spiritual consciousness never weeps; grief comes from the feeling of loss; spiritual consciousness knows that there is no loss; nothing ever can be lost; whatever was, is, and evermore shall be. To spiritual consciousness there are no tears; not because such consciousness is cold or indifferent, for he who has entered spiritual consciousness loves with a higher, a truer and a far more tender love than he ever knew before. He who has entered spiritual consciousness knows that all is well; and where all is well there can be no tears. Spiritual consciousness feels the existence, the presence and the unity of all things, visible and invisible. To be consciously in the spirit is to love all souls with the love of the spirit, and he who loves with the spirit is one with all souls, both in this realm and in realms beyond. He is conscious of the great white throng—those who are in the form and those who are in a higher form. His sublime love has given him a sublime vision, and through that vision he can see that nothing is lost, that all is well, and all that is well is eternal.

CHAPTER XXVI

The Supreme Purpose of Life

The beliefs of the past have told us that we are now living in time, and that later on we shall enter eternity; but we are rapidly discarding this idea; first, because it is not true, and second, because we have discovered this idea to be one of the chief causes of age and premature death. By premature death we mean the passing away from this sphere before we have fulfilled the purpose for which we came, and since we are here for some special purpose, we must permit nothing that will take us away before our work is finished.

That we are living here for some great purpose we must all admit; that we have something very important to accomplish in this world we are all beginning to learn; and that we must necessarily remain here for a long time to rightly promote the divine plan is becoming more and more evident. When we think of this great theme from every viewpoint of consciousness we invariably come to the conclusion that man should remain here until he reaches such a high spiritual state that nothing in the world of things can serve him any more; and we shall find that when we begin to live for the attainment of this sublime state, every moment of existence will be perfect bliss. It is truly sweet to live when we live to promote the great divine plan.

We find, however, that but very few live a good life and that only a limited number reach a high spiritual state before taking their departure. But what might the reason be? We all realize that old age is unnatural; and none of us require logic to demonstrate the great advantage of a life where eternal youth and eternal ascension in life are blended into one. Therefore we wish to find the fundamental cause of those conditions that produce age, that produce sickness, and that take us away from this sphere before our work is done. And this cause we find in the fact that man thinks he is living in time; when he should know that he is living in eternity.

When man fully realizes that he is living now in the great eternal now and that he is already in eternity, he shall know age no more. Man grows old because he believes in the passing of time. He believes that he is living in a world where time is ever going and that he is going with it, to the grave. He is conscious of the passing of years and believes that the further he goes with the years the more years will be added to the burden of his life. He therefore thinks of himself as so many years old; but here he is mistaken. Time is not passing; time is; and the time that is, is eternity.

What we call time is only that period in eternity that we are conscious of now, and in truth we cannot call it a period of any definite length. To some it is long, to others it is short, to some it passes quickly, to others it drags, and it is variously interpreted by various minds; but the time itself continues to be the same—the eternity that we are conscious of now. It may be stated, however, that time must be passing because something certainly does appear to come and go. But this is only the changing attitude of consciousness as man ascends in the scale. We look at the sun; it appears to move, but we know that the sun is not moving from the earth's point of view; it is the earth that is moving. In like manner, we have looked upon time as passing, but now we know that time is standing still; we are moving upward and onward forever.

When man becomes conscious of the fact that time is standing still, that he is moving, and that the further on he moves the larger his life becomes, he will have attained the secret of that life that is ever young. It may be stated, however, that if man believes he is moving, that belief will cause him to think of advancing age; but the truth is that when man realizes that he is ever moving onward he will know that he is growing into life; and he will never pass into age so long as he is growing into life.

The many believe that time is passing, coming to man and going away from man, and that man himself is passing, not into life but out of life; in consequence, the life more abundant is not realized. What the race does realize in growth, advancement and higher attainment is produced partly by the natural power of life to ascend in the scale and partly by the efforts of great souls. The race belief, however, concerning time and man's relation to time, is a constant obstacle, both to emancipation from the imperfections of the lesser life, and the ascension into greater life. To secure emancipation now, to realize that youthful life now that is a necessary part of the spiritual life, and to rise daily into the greater spiritual life, the usual conception of time must be reversed. But we cannot accomplish this by trying to change our relations to those external devices that measure the movements of nature; nor will a denial of nature avail in the least. The change that is required must take place in our own consciousness.

Realize that time is, that the time that is is eternity, and that eternity is still, always here, forever giving forth her riches to man. Realize that there is no time except the eternal; therefore time does not pass because there is neither time to pass nor passing time. Realize this great truth in the depths of consciousness, and years will only add to your power, your youth, your life and your spiritual attainments. Then you shall remain upon earth until your work is finished—until you have reached the Christ state.

When this truth is realized, you will consciously feel the stillness and the calm of the eternity that forever is. You will no longer feel that you are passing on and on to some undesired end where adverse forces will rob you of the life you are here to live; you will no longer think of death or those periods of inability that have formerly preceded death; these mean nothing to you; they do not belong to your life; you are living in eternity; time is not adding years to your life; your life is eternal, and that which is eternal cannot be measured by years. The movements of nature in their circles and spirals may be measured; but that has nothing to do with life or time. Nature is forever moving around the great eternal now, and the eternal now is living in the deep silence of the life that forever is now. The life that you live, the real life, the eternal life, is the same life that is now; and in that life there is no time, no years, no age, only eternity.

Ascension in life means the appropriation of more and more of real life; it does not mean the changing of life from one state to another, nor the passing through periods of time. Growth does not come from the passing of time; growth comes from appropriation; besides, there is no passing of time. When we think of growth we usually think of so much gain in so much time, but that is a mistake. The soul that truly lives, appropriates all that it needs each moment; no more, no less; it does not deal with time; it deals only with that which has real, eternal existence; it never thinks of tomorrow beecause in eternity there is no tomorrow; it lives now, and it knows that the life that is now will never pass away.

When we become conscious of eternal life we no longer question the immortal existence of the soul. To feel eternal life is to know that life is eternal and that every soul that lives, lives the life eternal now. We cannot separate the life of the soul from the life that is eternal, and the moment that we discover that the two are one we know that we shall live forever. We need no external demonstration to prove to us that those that have gone before are still alive; we now know that no soul can possibly cease to exist, and we spiritually discern the immortal existence of all the souls in the world. We seek no visible sign because we are in the presence of that something from which every sign must proceed. We no longer ponder over the life after death; we know there is no death. That which is eternal life can never die, and to beecome conscious of the soul is to discover that the soul is eternal life. The soul is coexistent with God; what God is the soul is; the soul is the real man, the man that is forever in the image and likeness of God.

When we ask "If a man die, shall he live again?" we prove to those who understand that we are still living in the person, and that we still think of ourselves as being persons. The person passes away, and therefore so long as we think that we are persons we think that we shall also pass away; but we are not certain whether we shall pass into nothingness or into another life;

we do not know because we are not awakened into that consciousness of eternal life that does know. We doubt no more, however, when we discover the real life of the soul and find that we are not persons but spiritual entities, sons of the Most High. If you wish to convince yourself that you are to live after you have removed the physical body, do not seek after mysterious signs in the without; seek rather the real life in the within. The more deeply you enter into real life the more fully you realize that there is no end to your own life. The outer consciousness informs you that you have life; the inner consciousness informs you that there is no end to your life, and the one is as convincing to the mind as the other.

You know that you are living because you are conscious of life. Enter more deeply into the reality of your being and you become conscious of eternal life. Then you will not only know that you are living, but you will know that there can be no end to your living. To be conscious of life is to know that you are living now; to be conscious of eternal life is to know that you are living in eternity now and that to live in eternity is to be eternal. To develop the consciousness of eternal life it is only necessary to grow daily in the spiritual life. Seek to understand the reality of your own divine being, and you will not only develop that spiritual discernment that knows the immortal existence of your own soul, but you will also develop that discernment that knows the present continued existence of all souls. You will know that you are destined to live eternally, and you will know that all souls, from ages past, are now living eternally. You know this, not through signs from without, or evidences that may appeal to physical senses or psychical senses, but through that spiritual understanding that is in conscious touch with every soul in God's unbounded cosmos. Neither the physical senses nor the psychical senses can know the soul; it is therefore impossible to demonstrate to any of those senses that the soul is immortal. Spiritual consciousness alone can know this great truth and to be spiritually conscious is to live in that sacred, interior realm where we know that man is perfect and divine, as God is perfect and divine. We know this when we are in the spirit, for nothing can be hidden in the light of the spirit. In that light we see all things as they are; therefore we know, and we speak with authority, not from ourselves but from God. In the spirit we are with God, and His thought becomes our thought, His word our word, His life our life.

When you see someone leaving the body you do not weep if you are spiritually awakened; you know that the leave-taking is but seeming; there is neither going nor coming in the spirit; there is no separation in spirit; in the spirit all are one in His love. Though the soul that seems to depart becomes invisible to physical sight, still that soul is ever visible to spiritual sight. To be consciously in the spirit is to see all those who live in the spirit whatever the form may be. In the consciousness of the spirit the manifestation of the form is secondary; whether the form be physical or ethereal is not of first importance; but to know the spirit, to be conscious of the spirit, and to know that all souls are eternally in the spirit—that is the first importance. That soul that seems to have gone, has not gone; you who are in the spirit, can feel her life, her presence and her love just the same; and you are wide awake to the fact that she still lives. Her existence is just as real to you as it was before, because in the spirit all is real. To you, who are in the spirit, all souls are real whether they manifest in this world or in some other world. They are all in God's sublime world, and when you are spiritually conscious your eyes are opened to the splendor and glory of that world.

CHAPTER XXVII

The Psalm of Rejoicing

The Lord is my shepherd; I shall not want.

When we are led by the spirit of the Most High, the condition of want is removed completely; which means that we shall want for nothing. There is nothing that we may need or desire for the living of a complete life that we shall not receive when the Lord is our shepherd. We shall have abundance in every domain of existence, and no matter how great our demands may be the adequate supply will always be at hand; provided, however, that our demands are in accord with the ascending life, the life that leads to the heights.

We are not required to place limitations upon our demands or desires; the Supreme is not limited in His power to supply; it is our privilege to desire everything that we may need to make life as large, as perfect, and as beautiful as we possibly can; in brief, the more we desire the greater becomes the life we live, and the greatest life is the most acceptable life to God as well as to man. We do not please God by humbling ourselves into insignificance, the Infinite does not ask us to be small because He is great; He does not demand that we be satisfied with little because He has everything. This is not the nature of God because God is love, and love eternally declares, "Be as I am; come and enjoy everything that I have to enjoy; what is mine is thine; what is for me is for thee, and nothing shall be withheld whatever."

To want for nothing means that we shall be in possession of everything—everything that is necessary to a life that is all that real life is intended to be. This means that we shall have all the peace that the soul may require, even the peace that passeth understanding; we shall have all the wisdom and all the power that we may need to attain in life whatever our highest aspirations may have in view; we shall have sufficient joy to satisfy perfectly every element in the whole of being; we shall have happiness without measure, harmony as beautiful as the symphonies of heaven, and health in perfection forever. Not a moment shall your body know any ailment whatever, and not a moment shall your mind know sorrow or pain. This is the truth. It could not be otherwise when the Lord is your shepherd. God is love, and love leads away from ills and pains into the infinite delights of sublime existence.

God is equal to all your needs; He can give health and strength to the body; He can give peace and power to the mind; He can give wisdom and joy to the soul; He can surround your personal life with all that is rich and beautiful in physical existence; He can surround your spiritual life with all that is gorgeous and sublime in cosmic existence; and when you select Him as your shepherd He will. Take God at His word. Do not believe in His goodness and power and then act as if your belief was not true. Believe that He will actually supply your every need, then act accordingly. Have faith in abundance and expect your faith to come true. You shall not be kept waiting, nor shall you long remain empty-handed. Your prayers shall be answered, your needs shall be supplied, and all that your life may require shall now become your own.

Do not depend upon yourself alone. The belief that man must depend wholly upon himself to rise to the heights of being is not true. Man alone can do nothing of real worth; it is only when we work with God and God works with us that we can do what the ideal within us desires to do. The greatest things in the world are done by those who constantly depend upon God, who walk with God and live with God, and then make the fullest, the largest and the best use of those powers they are eternally receiving from God. Wherever you may go, or whatever you may wish to do, take the Lord for your shepherd and you shall positively gain what you have in view. Failure becomes impossible because God is equal to any condition that may arise, and so long as you are with God, God is with you. Though you may meet adversity, you need not be disturbed; something will happen; God will cause something to happen so that things will take a turn; you shall be led into pastures green where all your desires shall be granted. Then you shall want for nothing. Remember, you shall want for nothing. This is the great truth to understand fully and demonstrate fully in the actual living of life.

The secret is absolute trust and faith in the goodness and the power of the Supreme. Believe that God is your shepherd; believe that you can want for nothing so long as He is with you; then act accordingly. Live as if you actually believed that your belief was true, and you shall find it to be true. It is only when we live the truth that the truth proves itself to be the truth. Do not wait for external evidence before you proceed to act upon your faith. Real faith has any amount of internal evidence, and any principle that proves itself to be true in the within can be demonstrated to be true in the without. What the vision of the soul may declare, the powers of the personal man can supply; and daily life can be made as true, as beautiful and as sublime as the life that is lived on the heights.

He maketh me to lie down in green pastures;
he leadeth me beside the still waters.

To be led by the spirit of the Most High is to pass through perpetual change, to pass from the good to the better, from the better to the best, and then higher and higher into those richer realms that infinite love has in store. In such a life there is always something new to live for, always something higher, something better to enjoy. Such a life can never be wearisome nor monotonous, for it is nothing less than a continuous feast, the richest imaginable feast, and all the elements of that feast are changed as often as we desire. It is in this feast that we partake of "the meat that ye know not of," and it is in this feast that the soul is nourished unto eternal life. Then comes the great spiritual strength that gives us the power to transcend the seeming and enter into the realms of existing sublime. And how beautiful to enter the pastures green of those lofty worlds, there to lie down and rest in the peace that passeth understanding, in the deep eternal calm that touches the soul with the symphonies of heaven. And how beautiful to be led beside the still waters, the living waters of celestial kingdoms on high, peacefully flowing onward and onward into that fairer kingdom, wherein we shall enter some golden morn, there to behold what eternity has in store for man.

When we follow the spirit, countless worlds are constantly opening before us, and in those worlds there are pastures green everywhere. In these we shall find nourishment for the soul; in these we shall find rest for the spirit. Then shall the soul come forth with new strength; then shall the spirit arise with power, and the spiritual life within us shall begin its great eternal reign. And when the spirit begins its reign, the outer world takes upon itself the peace, the wholeness, the harmony and the perfection of the beautiful life within. Adversity disappears; wrongs give place to the purity of the life divine; imperfections are lost in the dimness of the past, and the richness that we find in the pastures green, of realms sublime, is reproduced in personal existence. Then we shall realize in the without what the soul has discerned in the within; then the joys of the spirit shall be made known to the person, and life in this world shall become the image and likeness of that other life that our most lofty moments have so beautifully revealed.

When the Infinite leads you and guides you, you will constantly be led into the larger, the greater and the better. Pastures green will always be ready for you the very moment you are ready for a larger, richer life. You will never have to remain in the lesser for a single moment after you are ready for the greater; the Most High will open the way for you, and the increase you desire in your life shall speedily become your own. All the world rests upon the Great law of perpetual increase; and the pathway of all life is upward and onward forever; therefore to follow the law of life is to ever ascend into a greater and a greater measure of the highest good that life can give. The great law of life is the law of infinite life because God is the source of all law and all life; and since God lives as His own laws direct, we understand that when we follow the laws of life we shall live as He lives. And we always follow His laws when we are led by Him. We therefore conclude that all life that is led by the spirit of infinite life will ever live in perpetual increase. In such a life the greatest good in life will be enjoyed now, and that good will become higher and greater without any end.

The great truth to remember is that God always leads into the greater, never to the lesser. When the Lord is your shepherd you will eternally be led into pastures green, and every new pasture will be richer than the one you knew before. Walk with God; live in the presence and the power of His spirit and follow the light of the Supreme in all things; then you shall be led eternally into greater and greater things. The boundless will ever be at your door and your faith will open that door. This is a great truth; it is a truth that we must always remember and always apply because we can receive from infinite supply only what we believe that we will receive. Believe with heart and soul that you will receive everything that is necessary to the fullness and completeness of ideal living, and you will receive all these things if you have taken the Lord for your shepherd. He will lead you into pastures green, and your faith will open your life to all the richness that those newer worlds may contain.

The Infinite never leads into trouble, sickness, adversity or pain. When we enter such conditions we are not led by the spirit of the Most High; we are simply going away from His spirit, and thus create the very ills from which we soon must suffer. When we go away from God we create evil; this is the only way that evil can be created, and the evil we thus create is the only evil that can ever come to us. Therefore the one great remedy that can heal all the ills of human life is found in that wonderful statement, "Return Ye Unto God."

When people who claim to be spiritual are led into sickness and trouble, they are either mistaking emotionalism for spirituality, or their spirituality is as yet but a negative quality. When we begin to walk with God we begin to gain real spirituality, but such a spirituality is not simply a beautiful vision of the perfect and the divine; nor is it simply an aesthetic feeling or a tender sentiment; it is the great spiritual life within coming forth with living power. Spirituality is sweet and tender and beautiful, but it is also immensely strong. Therefore when we are in possession of real spirituality the ills of life must vanish just as darkness disappears with the coming of the light. No ill can exist in the living power of the spirit, and we are always filled through and through with that power when we are in the spirit, when we are living in that life that God lives. And when the Lord is our shepherd He invariably leads us into His life, His world, His kingdom, and into His light, wherein we shall know the truth, the truth that gives freedom to all that is in the being of man.

When you are led "beside the still waters" everything in your life will move smoothly, and all your efforts, experiences and modes of existence will work together harmoniously for greater and greater good. At first, or for some time, there may be conditions in your life that are not as they should be, but these will soon pass away, and while they do remain you will be so strong, if you live in God, that no adversity can disturb you in the least. When you are led by the spirit of the Most High, adversity will become less and less, while you will gain in strength, more and more, so that whatever adversity you may for a while meet will be as nothing in your life. You thus become able to master whatever may appear in the present, and you are, at the same time, rising out of every condition that is in any manner undesirable or adverse. You are led beside the still waters into the peace, the contentment and the joy of complete emancipation.

The life that is led by the spirit is the most peaceful, the most comfortable and the most sweetly serene of all life; it is ever beside the still waters, and is ever in touch with the great eternal calm. But it is also the most interesting as well as the most beautiful, for it is ever moving onward and onward. And here we find a great secret. The great life is not the life that imitates the storm-tossed sea, but the life that is deep and strong and yet always peaceful and still. Such a life is great in power, limitless in capacity and wonderful in efficiency, but in all things and at all times, is forever sweetly serene. Such a life sounds the very depth of real being and calmly brings to the surface the rich treasures of those inexhaustible realms within. And thus the entire domain of human existence is made larger, richer and more beautiful without any end. We shall ever find pastures green both in the within and in the without, and beside the still waters we shall be led into that peaceful life that we have sometimes felt when the soul was attuned to God.

He restoreth my soul; he leadeth me in the paths
of righteousness for his name's sake.

When we enter into the life of the Infinite, all that is high, all that is perfect and all that is beautiful in the soul will be restored to consciousness. The glory, the divinity and the sublime majesty of the soul will be revealed; the veil of mystery will be removed and we may behold the gorgeous splendor of the spiritual life as it truly is. The soul is no longer lost from view; we are no longer ignorant of the wonderful life within us; the heavens are opened, so to speak, and we may see most clearly and most perfectly that eternal something within us that is created in the image and likeness of God. Our divine nature is restored to us; we learn what we are; we discover our great inheritance; we find that we are not mere human creatures, but sons of the Most High, destined to reign with Him on the heights of glory and to live in His sublime kingdom during countless ages yet to be.

When the soul is restored, our inner spiritual nature becomes the ruling power in life; mind and body becomes servants to the soul, and we no longer live for circumstances, conditions and things; we begin to live for life itself, and we thus gain, in an ever increasing measure, all the richness, all the beauty and all the power that life can give. When we live for life we can gain everything of worth that is in life, and we invariably live for life when the soul is the ruling power in life. In the life of the soul all is perfect and all is well because the soul lives the same life that God lives. Therefore when the soul becomes the ruling power in personal life, we will live as God lives in our entire domain of life, and throughout that domain all will always be well. When the soul is the master in human life, all will be well in human life, and the soul is always restored to its high place in life when we elect to be led by the spirit of God.

The soul is perfect, being created in the image of God; therefore, the elimination of the imperfect in life must begin when the soul becomes the ruling power. When the soul rules in mind and body it will live in every part of mind and body; and where the soul lives there can be neither sickness nor pain, neither weakness nor want. When the soul is restored to its high place of majesty and power in life, all the ills of life must inevitably disappear. When the light returns, the darkness is no more. When the wholeness of the spirit becomes a living power in mind and body, the life of the person must necessarily become as clean, as strong and as wholesome as the life of the soul. And such a state of being is invariably secured when the soul is selected to reign in the wonderful kingdom of man. The ills of life come only when we follow those desires of the person that are not inspired from within; but when the soul is restored, every desire of the person will be true to the life of the spirit. We shall then no longer follow darkness into wrong and distress, but we shall follow divine light into peace, wholeness, freedom and joy. We naturally follow our desires in everything that we may think or do; therefore when all our desires are born from above, we shall naturally keep the eye single upon the light from above, and in consequence will even be led by the wisdom of God.

When the soul is restored to complete mastership in the human domain, everything changes for the better; a new life begins and all the elements of this new life contain possibilities for greater things than we ever knew before. We actually enter a new world, and the former things are passing away. What was against us either disappears or changes so completely that all its power is given to the promotion of what we have in view; and those things that always were for us become stronger and stronger until we feel that limitless power is on our side. When the soul rules the destiny of human life all the forces of life will build for a greater and a greater destiny; all things will move toward the heights; want will give place to perpetual increase; sickness will give place to wholeness and strength, and adversity will give place to harmony and joy. Restore the soul to mastery in your life and your entire being will be restored to its birthright divine; all that is worthy and beautiful in sublime existence will begin to accumulate in your world, and life to you will be rich indeed.

Follow the spirit and you will always go right. He will lead you in the paths of righteousness, and whatever you think or do will always be for the best. In brief, nothing but the best can happen to you because the Lord is your shepherd and He will surely care for His own. The spirit never leads into anything but that which is right, that which is good, that which is best. When you do not follow the spirit, you are either going wrong or you are drifting into channels that will finally take you into the wrong. You may not be consciously following the spirit now, and yet you may be seemingly going right now, but this does not mean that you are on the true path. Those who are not following the spirit now are going wrong, and to them adversity will come sooner or later. Present conditions, however favorable, do not prove that you are on the path that leads to freedom and the greater life. You are on that path only when you know that you are led by His spirit in all things and at all times. We cannot judge according to appearances; the truth comes only from the supreme light within; and when we know the truth and live accordingly, we know that all will be right. I in the within and in the without, all will be right.

We all follow the inner light to some degree; the soul is awakened in us all and is prompting us all; but in many instances we are led by those personal desires that are not in harmony with real life, and we are influenced by external conditions and things; thus we go wrong, and here is the cause of our troubles and pains. Whenever we go right, we go right because we have followed the higher promptings from within; and whenever we go wrong, we go wrong because we have followed those external conditions that are not in harmony with the real life within. But do we know when we are prompted by the soul? Do we know when we are led by the spirit? Do we know when we are guided by the Infinite and by Infinite Wisdom alone? At first we may not know; we may follow the spirit at times without knowing that it is the spirit, and at times we may think we are led by the spirit and yet be mistaken. But every person who fully and absolutely decides to follow the spirit in all things, henceforth and forever, will not long remain unconscious to the radiant presence of the Most High. If you will take this great step your spirit will soon be attuned to the tender music of the still small voice, and your mind will be illumined more and more with the glory of His sight. Then you will know, and never be mistaken, whenever He speaks to you; then you will see His light at all times and you will always know that it is the light divine. You will readily discern the meaning of His will in all things, and you will find that to follow His will is to go where glory is waiting. Not to some other world, but to His world, here and now. "There is another and a better world" here and now wherein we all may dwell in the never-ending today; and the light of His spirit leads directly into the freedom and joy of that beautiful world.

> *Yea, though I walk through the valley of the*
> *shadow of death, I will fear no evil:*
> *For thou art with me;*
> *thy rod and thy staff they comfort me.*

When God is with us nothing but that which is good can happen. It matters not what we may meet or what we may be required to pass through, good will be the final outcome. We need fear no condition that can possibly arise; Supreme Power is with us, and we may overcome and surmount anything. We shall come out of every experience uninjured and unharmed; nothing can hurt us because there can be no hurt in the presence of infinite goodness, infinite power, infinite love. Wherever we are called we may safely go; whatever we are expected to do we may proceed. So long as we feel and know that God is with us, all will be well. We shall be led, guided, directed and protected; we may, without doubt or fear, proceed to do our part, and leave results to higher power; the very best will come to pass. Even though things happen for a short time that seem adverse, the outcome of everything will be good, very good. The light of divine wisdom is guiding our life, our thought, our actions, our destiny, and therefore all things will work together for the very highest good that we can possibly realize in every state of continued existence.

What is here spoken of as the valley of the shadow of death is the most extreme condition of danger that a person can possibly pass through; there can be no worse state of threatening calamity than the "dark valley," yet even there "I will fear no evil, for thou art with me." It matters not to what extreme we may be taken by circumstances or fate, God is equal to all our needs. He can protect us and guide us anywhere, and He will. He can take us out in safety, and He will surely do so if we have selected Him as our shepherd. And not simply because His power is supreme, but also because where God is there can be no evil. There is no evil to fear where God is because there can be no evil where God is. Be with God and God will be with you; and when God is with you, you are ever in the presence of the good and the beautiful. You are in a world where freedom is complete, where truth is omnipresent, and where all the elements of life are in touch with higher and better things.

When we are in the presence of danger we almost invariably shrink into dread or fear of some kind; and when called upon to do what seems beyond us, or what we personally dislike, we usually hesitate, or refuse absolutely; but this is all a mistake. God is with us; we need fear nothing, for He will protect us in everything. God is our strength, and with His strength we can surely do anything that life may require of us. When we feel weak we should remember that His rod and His staff are at our service. If we must have something to lean upon, His staff is ever at hand, and with such a staff we shall not fall down; no matter how heavy the burden, or how difficult the task, we shall not fall down. His staff will support us whenever we may need support; His rod will hold us up whatever the circumstances may be, and the power of His presence will give us all the strength we may require to reach any goal we may have in view. We should rather look upon difficulties as opportunities through which we may demonstrate to others the great truth that nothing is impossible when God is with us. And when called upon to do what seems beyond our capacity, we shall proceed nevertheless, pressing on in the full faith that we can. God is with us, and when He is with us we can do anything that our present sphere of existence may require.

If we have a great purpose to carry through we need never hesitate. Though the opposition may be great and the obstacles seemingly insurmountable, we may safely proceed. We need fear neither danger nor defeat, for Thou art with me. God will see us through. The Lord is our shepherd; we shall want for nothing; indeed, we shall receive everything we may need to accomplish what we have undertaken. When the task seems hard and the flesh seems weak, then we should remember, Thy rod and Thy staff they comfort me. And in that comfort our strength shall return, even more than enough to carry through the task that lies before us. We are equal to any occasion when God is with us, and God will always be with us if that is our deepest prayer of the heart. Therefore, we should never complain, and never give up to weariness or defeat. When it seems as if we could do nothing more, God will do the rest; and if we take heart again and proceed in unison with Him, we shall become stronger than we ever were before. When it seems as if everything would be lost, we should refuse to judge according to the seeming.

"The Lord is my shepherd." The seeming loss will not take place. The tide will turn. God can turn anything in our favor, and if we accept Him as our shepherd He always will.

When God is our strength how great indeed is that strength. With Him at our side we have our own life in our own hands, and may do with it whatsoever we will. The present is ours to enjoy, the future is ours to create. Adverse indications mean nothing; threatening ills or failures mean nothing; we need fear none of these things. God is greater than all outward indications, and His greatness is with us, on our side, working for our happiness and welfare. We should never recognize that which seems to be against us, for when God is with us His strength is our strength, His life is our life, and the wisdom that illumines His mind the same wisdom shall illumine our minds also. We therefore can never have any occasion to fear, to hesitate or to entertain doubts in any form or manner. The Lord is our shepherd. He will surely care for His own, and whatever is necessary to give fullness, perfection and completeness to the great eternal now, that we shall all receive.

God is with us when we choose to be with God. This is the simple secret. When we select Him as our shepherd, then we become His own; then He will care for us, guide us and protect us; then He will place the gates ajar so we may enter into pastures green; then He will lead us beside the still waters into the peace and the joy of the beautiful life. It will all be as we desire. The Infinite is ever ready, and it is our privilege to accept His goodness today. But to accept Him as our shepherd does not mean that we must completely relinquish our own will and our own way. When we decide to go God's way we shall find that He is helping us to gain our way; and when we decide to follow His will we shall find that He is giving us all the power required to carry out our will. Thus we shall find that the goodness of God is far greater than we thought and that His love is as boundless as the infinite sea.

Thou preparest a table before me in the presence of mine enemies: Thou anointest my head with oil; my cup runneth over.

When God is with us we shall continue to enjoy the best that life can give regardless of what surrounding conditions may be. Though things may seemingly be against us and though we may be in the presence of enmity and adversity; nevertheless those things shall neither touch us nor disturb us. In the midst of such circumstances, or any kind of circumstances, God will prepare a table of everything that is rich and desirable in life. Whatever may happen in the world in which we live, God will protect us from loss. His table will always be richly laden, and it will be our privilege to partake according to our largest and most heartfelt need. When the Lord is our shepherd we need fear neither persons nor things that may seem to be against us. When God is with us, nothing can be against us. We have a place at His table, and those who are guests at His table shall want for nothing. He will provide for His guests and provide richly; therefore if we accept Him as our everlasting host we need never be disturbed about any condition, circumstance or event. The best will happen, and all will always be well.

When things go wrong with those who are living only for the world, things will go right with us. Misfortune cannot overtake us. In His presence the power of evil is powerless, and we are ever in His presence so long as we elect that we so shall be. When we take God with us, and leave all our plans and desires with God before we decide, there will not even be indications of misfortune or adversity in our world. He will continue to prepare His table before us, and we shall continue to enjoy, both the good things of this world, and "the meat that ye know not of." We shall continue in prosperity even though all who live in the material world go down into adversity. The Lord is our shepherd, and we shall not want. However, if we should meet what would seem to be the indications of a threatening misfortune, we need not be disturbed. There may be temporary losses, and adverse conditions may come so near as to almost enter into our very lives, nevertheless we need not be disturbed. Whatever may threaten to happen, we need fear no evil, for Thou art with me. The entire experience will simply prove to be an open door to better things and greater things than we ever knew before. Such experiences sometimes come to those who are in His care; not often, but sometimes; and they come to test our faith, our spiritual strength and our dependence upon Him; they come to prepare us for a greater life, for pastures green, for new fields of endeavor and for a higher mission in the world. Count it all joy; so long as we are with God, God will be with us; and He will cause all things to work together for greater good than we ever dreamed.

Whatever may come to the world, the best alone can come to us. And we shall thus not only realize the richness and the beauty of that life that is lived in God, but we shall become living examples to the world, proving to the world that God's way is best. We shall then demonstrate to all who have eyes to see, that to follow the light of the spirit is to follow that light that leads into everything that is worthy and beautiful in endless existence. The world believes that the spiritual life leads away from happiness and abundance; we must prove to everybody that the spiritual life leads into greater happiness and a richer life than we have ever known before. And we can prove this when we take the Lord for our shepherd. When we accept a place at His table, we shall demonstrate in the most tangible and the most convincing manner that to go with God is to go where every person may supply his every need; and not only be supplied, but supplied in the richest, the most worthy and the most ideal manner conceivable. To go with God is to find everything that heart can wish for in this world, and in addition, the infinite glory, the gorgeous splendor and the supreme joy of His kingdom on the heights.

To be anointed with oil is to have everything that is worthy and superior come down upon us. The oil of all things is the richest essence of all things, and when we are anointed with this richest essence, our minds become enriched with all that has quality and worth, all that is high in the scale of being. And it is but natural that that mind that lives and thinks with God, should be constantly enriched. Everything that comes from God has quality; everything that we receive from God has high worth, and everything that pertains to the spiritual life contains all the elements of real superiority; therefore, to follow God is to rise eternally in the scale of superior being. When we elect to go with God we leave behind us all that is common, ordinary or inferior; and we put on the royal garments of true quality and high worth. We become superior in body, mind and soul, and every element in our being becomes a living expression of that quality that reveals the royal presence of God.

When we are actually living in the spirit, and can fully appreciate all that is good and beautiful in real life, we become so filled with gratitude and joy that neither thoughts nor words can express what we feel. It is then that we wish as never before "that the mind could fathom and the tongue could utter the thoughts that arise in me." Our cup is running over; we have everything that can fill the fullness of life with the richness of life, and our joy is great indeed. Words fail us, but that something within that is far more eloquent than words gives utterance to what we wish to say. And as we listen, this language divine becomes heavenly music, repeating again and again that tender refrain, "God's beautiful gift to me."

To always live in the realization of that sublime state of being where our cup is running over is to become conscious more and more of the great truth that real life has everything that man can wish for, and infinitely more. And as we grow in the conscious realization of this truth, the power of this truth will manifest itself in our external world. Then we shall find increase everywhere; wherever we may go in the physical world, in the mental world or in the spiritual world, God will prepare His table before us, and we shall enjoy the richest feast that His infinite goodness can possibly provide. In every domain of existence His bountiful hand will be our supply, and our cup will always be running over. What we feel and realize in the world of the spirit, that we shall gain in the world of things. Thus our joy becomes complete; all that we need is always at hand, all that we desire for a greater existence shall be speedily supplied, and wherever our place in life may be, God will appear and prepare His table before us. He will be our supply always and everywhere; and existence will be rich indeed.

Surely goodness and mercy shall follow me all the days of my life; and I will dwell in the house of the Lord forever.
—PSALMS 23.

When the soul enters the faith that leads eternally into the kingdom, the entire being of man is placed in the keeping of the spirit of goodness. That power that works for the good and the good only, will henceforth be with man under every circumstance and condition; and all his actions will be attended by the angel of mercy. His life will be lived in the consciousness of the Infinite presence, and this consciousness is the open door to the house of the Lord. The moment we feel that God is closer than breathing, nearer than hands and feet, we are upon the threshold of the sublime spiritual world, the Father's House of the Many Mansions, and from that moment we may dwell in His house forever. From that moment all will be changed; life will never seem ordinary, commonplace or mere existence any more; we have seen the House Beautiful, we have felt the touch of the life that God lives, we have been on the heights, and we have had a glimpse of the glory that eternity holds in store. Henceforth, there is so much to live for, that simply to think of the ever ascending destiny that lies before us, is in itself a source of unspeakable joy. Then who can measure the peace, the joy—in brief, the unbounded ecstasy that must follow the living of the life? Those who have been led beside the still waters know the meaning of such a life. Those who have entered the house of the Lord know what is prepared for them that love Him. But tongue can never tell, and only the mind of the soul can understand.

To follow the spirit is to enter the glorified vastness of the great spiritual mind within; and here is wisdom. Spiritual things must be spiritually discerned; we must enter spiritual light in order to know the reality of our own divine being, and the mind of the soul is eternally illumined with this light. There are no mysteries in spiritual consciousness; all is clear; the meaning of life is perfectly understood; the purpose of it all is distinctly revealed, and the soul knows what it is about every step of the way. Every soul that goes with God in all things and at all times will ever live in this consciousness, and will ever rise higher and higher into the greater brilliancy and the more sublime beauty of the spiritual light. To live such a life is to dwell in the house of the Lord, and whosoever will may dwell in that house forever.

The world in which we live may not, at present, contain everything that the heart can wish for; but "there is another and a better world" that does contain everything. Our human dwelling place may not be perfect, it may not be complete, it may not satisfy the soul's longing for the ideal and the beautiful; but the house of the Lord can satisfy. We therefore need not be unhappy; personal life need not be incomplete because there are seeming limitations among external conditions. The fact that we manifest in visible form does not mean that we should live wholly among visible things. The law of true being is to manifest in the personal but to always live in the spiritual. The house of the Lord is our true dwelling place now and forever. And as there are many mansions in the Father's House, innumerable mansions, we shall not be confined to one place, or one state of existence; we shall live in each of these mansions; we shall enjoy them all, we shall pass through them all as eternity goes on. No matter how lofty the present abode of the soul, there is always something higher; no matter how unspeakable our spiritual joys today, or any time in eternity, there are always greater joys coming in days that are yet to be. We thus realize what it means to dwell in the house of the Lord forever.

When we have entered to dwell permanently in the house of the Lord, existence, both personal and spiritual, becomes perpetual joy. Whatever external conditions may be, or whatever may come and go in personal life, we are always in the joy everlasting, in the peace that passeth understanding, in the world on high where all is forever well. We no longer depend upon things, and we are no longer moved by things; we have transcended the world of things; we have gained the power to perfectly use things, and we are attaining the mastery of all things. We are living in God's world, the world of limitless richeness, happiness and power; therefore, the world of things constitutes but a small part of our vast and wonderful domain. We have found so many sources of joy, so many states of being that can add to the value of life, that though other things should sometimes fail, we are never affected in the least. Confusion and failure in the outer world mean no more to us than the loss of a penny would mean to a man who owns a mountain of gold. Things may come and go in the outer world, but we are living in the house of the Lord. In that house there is never confusion, trouble nor pain; in that house there can be neither failure nor want. The Most High provides for that house; therefore so long as we dwell in His house we shall want for nothing. Whatever may come or go, we shall always have abundance, both in the within and in the without. We need fear nothing; we may rejoice always, for in His house all is well, and for evermore shall be.

Dream on fair soul, dream on. Thy visions are not in vain. Other and greater worlds are waiting for thee. Dream on fair soul, dream on. Let thy spirit ascend to the supreme heights of those greater worlds where thou shalt behold the glory and splendor of that sublime existence that is in store for thee. And let nothing that may come or go in thy waking hours cause thee to forget what thou hast seen. For the time is near when the dreams of the night shall rise with the morning but shall not depart with the setting sun. What thou hast seen in thy visions shall come to remain; and what thy lofty moments have revealed to thee shall become thine own forever.

CHAPTER XXVIII

God's Beautiful Gift to Me

The great goal is cosmic consciousness, and every soul that endeavors to live according to the highest light that is known in the world is daily drawing nearer and nearer to that sublime state. To such a soul the heavens may be opened at any time, and the splendors of the cosmic world revealed. Then everything will change. Life will not be the same any more. The meaning of it all will be discerned, and no fault can be found anywhere. When we look at life from the heights of the cosmic realm we can see only the divine side of existence; we therefore can see no evil; in brief, when we are in the cosmic we have absolutely forgotten everything about evil; we do not know that there is such a thing as evil because we are in that exalted world where we can be conscious only of the good. And here is the real evidence of cosmic consciousness. When you have entered the peace that passeth understanding and the joy that can only be described as a million heavens in one, you are in the cosmic state, providing you have forgotten every ill and every wrong you ever knew. In the cosmic world everything is as God made it; nothing has been changed in any way; absolute perfection and absolute divinity reign supremely, and the glory of it all no power in man can ever attempt to picture. It is beyond all the powers of the personal man; it is for the soul only to understand and enjoy.

When we enter the cosmic state we transcend that part of man that takes cognizance of the imperfect and incomplete; we enter a realm that never knew anything less than absolute, divine perfection, and therefore when we are in that realm we can know no evil. In the cosmic state our eyes are too pure to see evil, and the mind too high in divine consciousness to even think of evil. We are thinking the thoughts of the Infinite and everything we are conscious of is manifesting the shining glory of the Most High. In the cosmic state we think the truth, the absolute truth, because in that state everything is the expression of absolute truth. Therefore, the more frequently we enter into the realization of cosmic consciousness the more fully will the mind discern the truth, and the more readily can we think the truth whatever the field of our thought may be.

There are many minds that think that they have frequent experiences in cosmic consciousness, but not all of these have judged those experiences correctly. The great within is filled with wonderful realms of every description, and some have mistaken one or more of these realms for the home of the soul when the body has been removed. Many have thought they have seen heaven after beholding the gorgeous splendor of these inner realms, while others, after meeting the beautiful thoughts that take human shape in the great within, believe they have conversed with angels. But this is not the cosmic world. Though we may find peace and joy and ecstasy without measure in many of these beautiful interior realms, still we also find imperfection in one or more of its many forms. We do not forget evil while we are in the ecstasy of the great within; nor do we become unconscious of everything but that which is pure shining divinity. This, however, is precisely what happens when we are in the cosmic state; we meet only that which is wholly in the likeness of God, and our joy at times becomes so great that our feelings cannot contain themselves. Our cup overflows and the person bursts forth in tears. We have found that for which we have waited and prayed so long; we are inwardly moved as never before, and it is but natural that the person should weep for joy. We have found eternal life, we have felt His presence, we have touched the hem of His garment, we have met Him face to face.

The greater number of those who are spiritually inclined are almost constantly on the verge of the cosmic state, and at intervals they receive glimpses of that wondrous world. Could they but see themselves at such moments, they would discover that their faces are also shining as the sun, for their minds are illumined with radiant glory from on high. But such moments do not usually come when the senses expect them, nor can they be produced at will. We gain glimpses of the cosmic only when the soul occupies the supreme state in consciousness, and we begin to live within the pearly gates of the cosmic when the soul has gained full supremacy in every domain in consciousness. Therefore, to attain cosmic consciousness, we must give the spiritual life the first place in everything; we must do everything to the glory of God and follow the light of the spirit in everything we may think or do. The eye must be single, and to see and to know only that which is wholly divine must be the one supreme desire.

The ruling spirit in the cosmic world is divine perfection; therefore the more we think of divine perfection, and the more we try to see divine perfection in all things, the more we develop the consciousness of divine perfection; and the development of this form of consciousness will finally culminate in divine consciousness which is synonymous with cosmic consciousness. To keep the eye single upon the great truth that every creation of God is good is to draw nearer and nearer to that state where we became conscious only of the absolutely good; then follows the limitless joy of the cosmic world. But when we permit the eye to become double, and begin to see the evil as well as the good, the unreal as well as the real, we fall from our lofty state; and this is the only fall of man. When we partake of the fruit from the tree of the knowledge of good and evil, we fall from the cosmic world, and we have to leave paradise. We cannot live in the garden of bliss, in the joys of cosmic consciousness, so long as we know evil as well as good; but when we become unconscious of evil, with the eye single upon His supreme goodness alone, then the gates of paradise shall open for us once more. Then we shall forget everything but that which is good and beautiful and true; we shall enter the new heaven and the new earth, the new heaven in the within, and the new earth in the without, and while still in personal form we shall live in the cosmic world.

To rise daily into a higher and better understanding of the reality of the cosmic state of existence is to become conscious, more and more, of the real sweetness of existence. Life becomes so rich and so beautiful that to live is in itself absolutely sufficient. In the cosmic state every moment seems to be an eternity of bliss, and every movement of consciousness produces a million pleasures. In comparison, the joys of sense have no significance whatever. Therefore, when the mere living of life gives all the joy that heart and soul may desire, it is evidence conclusive that the cosmic state has been reached; and the joys that are to follow, the soul on the heights alone can know.

The cosmic world is that highly refined, spiritualized world all about us, permeating everything, encompassing everything; the great divine sea in which we live and move and have our being; a world of pure light, gorgeous splendor and celestial brilliancy. The cosmic world is the world sublime; it is everywhere, and we live in it now and eternally, but only those who are spiritually awakened can discern its reality and behold the shining glories of its fair transcendent realms. When the true spiritual awakening begins we discover the cosmic world, and we enter cosmic consciousness. The heavens are opened and the vision before us reveals splendors and glories that tongue can never describe, joys that cannot be measured, and life that is a million heavens in one.

When we are in the cosmic state the entire world is clothed with the sun; the waters of the deep reflect the radiant glory of celestial kingdoms, and the mountains proclaim the majesty and the power of the life that is lived on the heights. Nature sings the everlasting praises of Him who is closer than breathing, nearer than hands and feet, and every human countenance beams with the beautiful smile of God. The flowers declare the thoughts of the Infinite; the forest chants the silent prelude to worship, while the birds inspire the soul to ascend to the vast empyrean blue. We are speechless with ecstasy, but as we behold the beauty and glory of it all the spirit within speaks from out the fullness of the heart and sweetly proclaims in language divine "God's beautiful gift to me."

There is an upper realm in the spiritual life of man where the reality and perfection of divine existence is revealed. In this realm all is truth, all is purity, all is love. To enter this realm is to become conscious of eternal truth and understand the truth as it manifests everywhere. In the cosmic state the spiritual understanding of truth is complete; therefore every step in the spiritual understanding of truth is a step toward cosmic consciousness. All understanding is spiritual that discerns the spirit of truth as well as the reality of truth; and the mind develops in the discernment of truth when every effort to understand truth enters into the very innermost life of truth. When you think of truth, think of the spirit of truth; that is, that spiritual life or soul that is within truth; and desire with all the power of life, thought and feeling to enter into the soul of truth. To enter into the soul of truth is to enter into the cosmic state, and you not only gain an illumined understanding of the truth itself, but you become conscious of the entire cosmic world. The heavens are opened, for I Am the door, the way, the truth, the spirit of truth.

To enter the cosmic state is to become conscious of that divinity within us that is too pure to behold anything but that which is absolute purity. "To the pure all things are pure," and in the cosmic state we become pure; we enter into the world of shining purity; we do not recognize evil, and to us, iniquity has no significance whatever. While we are in the cosmic state we are in a pure state and can know only the boundless world of sublime purity that is all about us and all within us everywhere. Therefore, to enter the cosmic state the mind must be pure; that is, the mind must face the divinity that is in all things and must, at all times, keep the eye single upon the shining purity of that divinity.

The cosmic realm is filled through and through with love, and to enter this realm is to love every living creature with all the power of heart and soul. When you are in the cosmic state you are in the universal; all life is divine to you; all life is beautiful, all life is precious, all life is sacred; your sympathy is as large as the universe and as touching as the innermost tenderness of the soul. To love everybody, no matter what they are or what they have done, is a part of your own life. You are above personal conditions; you are above personal deeds; you can see through the imperfect and behold the shining glory that reigns supremely in all that is. You see the divine reality in all things and you love it with all the tenderness of heart and soul. This divine loveliness in all things is the all in all in all things; to you it is beautiful, "fairer than ten thousand to the soul."

To love in the spirit of the universal is not to disregard the person. You love the person infinitely more because when you are in the cosmic every atom in the person is glorified with the presence of Him who is closer to life than breathing, nearer than hands and feet. You love the person because all that is true in that person is the coming forth of the divine. That which may not be true you do not see; your eyes are too pure to behold iniquity; besides, the imperfect in any person is insignificant and does not belong to the real person himself. Even in the most sinful of persons the evil is but a fragment compared with the good that is inherent in every fibre of his being. Take the worst person in the world and you will find the good and the right in him a thousand times greater than the wrong. When you are awakened to the truth you know this; therefore it becomes so easy to love; and since your heart is simply overflowing with love, you must love, love everything and everybody. And what a supreme joy is found in such a love.

To enter the cosmic state and develop cosmic consciousness, the soul must be given perfect freedom to love in the universal. It is a part of the life of the soul to love everything in existence; therefore the physical senses must not interfere with this love by impressing the mind to think that some things are evil and not worthy of love. Everything is worthy of love because in everything the good is infinitely greater than that which appears not to be good. The senses must be trained to recognize this great truth and the mind must be trained to harmonize all thinking with the sublime desires of the soul. When you meet a person see the all in all in that person; you will then see the shining purity of divine loveliness animating every fibre of his being; his countenance will be glorified before you, and you will love him with that beautiful love that reigned in the tenderness of the Christ. Meet all things in this sublime spiritual attitude, and the material veil will be removed more and more until all the splendors of the cosmic world are revealed to your vision.

To develop cosmic consciousness, place yourself in the hands of higher power. Depend upon higher power in all things; do nothing without first calling upon higher power; and so live that every thought, word and action is inspired by the spirit of higher power. Feel that higher power is always with you; deeply desire higher power to direct you, and open consciousness so completely to the limitless life of higher power that you actually realize that you live, move and have your being in the infinite power of the Most High. To enter the cosmic state you must transcend all belief in limitations; you must enter the universal where you clearly discern that all things are possible, for God is everywhere; and when your life is filled through and through with the presence of higher power you are lifted to the mountain tops of this lofty state. You rise above personal conditions and enter the limitless—where life is limitless, where power is limitless, where truth is limitless, where light is limitless, where the good is limitless, where love is limitless, where everything is limitless; and that is the cosmic world.

To live by faith is another supreme essential in the attainment of this sublime state. It is the very nature of faith to go out upon the limitless, and wherever faith may go, better things, higher things and greater things are found than were ever known before. Faith invariably leads upward and onward; faith always inspires the soul to ascend; while the spirit of faith illumines the way. To enter into the true spirit of faith, have faith in the innermost life of faith. There is a hidden power in faith; this power is the power of the Infinite; it is the soul of faith, the spirit of faith, and is eternally one with the spirit of the Most High. To enter into the spirit of faith is to enter into the spirit of the Most High, and thus be filled through and through with the power of the Most High. And this is the reason why all things are possible to him who has faith.

When you use the power of faith, have faith with the spirit of faith. You thus enter into the real power of faith and the illumined world of faith. In consequence, you not only gain the power to make all things possible, but you also enter into the spiritual light, and in the spiritual light the shining glory of the cosmic is revealed. To have faith with the spirit of faith, think of that supreme spiritual life and power that is in faith. Mentally dwell upon this inner life of faith, and whenever you use your faith, which should be every moment of existence, enter into the spirit of faith with all the power of feeling, thought and soul. You thus place yourself in perfect spiritual touch with the world of celestial light, with the world of divine wisdom, with the world of eternal life, with the world of limitless power, with the world of shining purity, with the world of that love that loves everything and everybody with the most touching tenderness of the Most High. You are in the Mind that was in Christ Jesus; you are in the same Spirit that He was when His face did shine as the sun and His garment became white as the light.